MANAGING FOR RESULTS

Other books by Peter F. Drucker

Management

Post-capitalist Society
Managing for the Future
Managing the Non-profit Organization
The Frontiers of Management
Innovation and Entrepreneurship
Management: Tasks, Responsibilities, Practices
The Effective Executive
The Practice of Management
The Changing World of the Executive
Managing in Turbulent Times
The New Markets and Other Essays
Concept of the Corporation

Economics, politics, society

The New Realities
Toward the Next Economics
The Unseen Revolution
Men, Ideas and Politics
The Age of Discontinuity
The Landmarks of Tomorrow
America's Next Twenty Years
The New Society
The Future of Industrial Man
The End of Economic Man

Fiction

The Temptation to Do Good
The Last of All Possible Worlds

Autobiography

Adventures of a Bystander

Managing for Results

Economic Tasks and
Risk-taking Decisions

PETER F. DRUCKER

Oxford   Auckland   Boston   Johannesburg   Melbourne   New Delhi

Butterworth-Heinemann
Linacre House, Jordan Hill, Oxford OX2 8DP
225 Wildwood Avenue, Woburn, MA 01801-2041
A division of Reed Educational and Professional Publishing Ltd

A member of the Reed Elsevier plc group

First published 1964
First published as a paperback edition 1989
Reprinted 1994 (twice), 1996
Reissued with new cover 1999

British Library Cataloguing in Publication Data
Drucker, Peter F. (Peter Ferdinand), *1990-*
Managing for results
1. Business firms. Management
I. Title
658

ISBN 0 7506 4391 9

Printed and bound in Great Britain by MPG Books Ltd, Bodmin, Cornwall

FOR EVERY TITLE THAT WE PUBLISH, BUTTERWORTH-HEINEMANN
WILL PAY FOR BTCV TO PLANT AND CARE FOR A TREE.

Contents

Acknowledgement

This book owes much to the editorial assistance given by my wife, Doris, and by my friend, Hermine Popper. Each read the manuscript several times and at several stages – for sense and sequence as well as for style, diction, and sentence structure. Their sensitivity to a misplaced thought and their intolerance of a misplaced word are in large measure responsible for whatever clarity, conceptual or textual, this book possesses. I am all the more grateful for their help as both interrupted urgent and important work of their own to read and edit *Managing for Results*.

New Year's Day 1964   PETER F. DRUCKER
Montclair, New Jersey

Introduction:
The Task

This is a 'what to do' book. It deals with the economic tasks that any business has to discharge for economic performance and economic results. It attempts to organize these tasks so that executives can perform them systematically, purposefully, with understanding, and with reasonable probability of accomplishment. It tries to develop a point of view, concepts and approaches for finding what should be done and how to go about doing it.

This book draws on practical experience as a consultant to businesses of all kinds and sizes for a good many years. Everything in it has been tested and is being used today effectively in real businesses. There are illustrations of, and references to, concrete situations on almost every page – drawn mostly from the United States (simply because most of my experience has been here) but also from Europe, Japan and Latin America.*

Though practical rather than theoretical, the book has a thesis. Economic performance, it asserts, is the specific function and contribution of business enterprise, and the reason for its existence. It is work to obtain economic performance and results. And work, to yield results, has to be thought through and done with direction, method and purpose. There is, however, so far, no discipline of economic performance, no organization of our knowledge, no systematic analysis, no purposeful approach. Even the sorting out and classification of the tasks have yet to be done. The foundation for systematic, purposeful performance of the specific task and function of business enterprise is thus still missing.

There are a good many successful businesses and effective executives – as there are many with at best mediocre results. One searches in vain, however, for an analysis that identifies what the successful are doing to give them results. Nowhere is there a description even of the economic tasks that confront a business, let alone how one goes about tackling them. To every executive's

* Wherever a company is mentioned by name the illustration is taken from published material, primarily company statements. Where no company name appears the example comes out of my own practice or observation and has been carefully disguised as to kind of business, size, location, products, and so on.

desk come dozens of problems every morning, all clamouring for his attention. But there is little to tell him which are important and which merely noisy.

This book lays little claim to originality or profundity. But it is, to my knowledge, the first attempt at an organized presentation of the economic tasks of the business executive and the first halting step towards a discipline of economic performance in business enterprise.

The book is divided into three parts. The first – and longest – stresses analysis and understanding. Chapter 1 deals with the 'Business Realities' – the situation most likely to be found in any business at any given time. The next three chapters (Chapters 2, 3 and 4) develop the analysis of the result areas of the entire business and relate them to resources and efforts on the one hand and to opportunities and expectations on the other. Chapter 5 projects a similar analysis on the cost stream and cost structure – both of the individual business and of the economic process of which it is part.

Chapters 6 and 7 deal with the understanding of a business from the 'outside' where both the results and the resources are. These chapters ask, 'What do we get paid for?' and 'What do we earn our keep with?' In Chapter 8 all analyses are pulled together into an understanding of the existing business, its fundamental economic characteristics, its performance capacity, its opportunities and its needs.

Part II focuses on opportunities and leads to decisions. It discusses the opportunities and needs in each of the major economic dimensions of a business: making the present business effective (Chapter 9); finding and realizing business potential (Chapter 10); making the future of the business today (Chapter 11).

The last – and shortest – part presents the conversion of insights and decisions into purposeful performance. This requires that key decisions be made regarding the idea and objectives of the business, the excellences it needs, and the priorities on which it will concentrate (Chapter 12). It requires a number of strategic choices: what opportunities to pursue and what risks to assume; how to specialize and how to diversify; whether to build or to acquire; and what organization is most appropriate to the economics of the business and to its opportunities (Chapter 13). Chapter 14 finally embeds the entrepreneurial decisions for performance in the managerial structure of the organization – in work, in business practices, and in the spirit of the organization and its decisions on people.

The 'Conclusion' projects the book and its thesis on the individual executive and his commitment – and especially on the commitment of top management.

Any first attempt at converting folklore into knowledge, and a guessing game into a discipline, is liable to be misread as a down-grading of individual ability and its replacement by a rule book. Any such attempt would be nonsense, of course. No book will ever make a wise man out of a donkey or a genius out of an incompetent. The foundation in a discipline, however, gives to today's competent physician a capacity to perform well beyond that of the ablest doctor of a century ago, and enables the outstanding physician of today to do what the medical genius of yesterday could hardly have dreamt of. No discipline can lengthen a man's arm. But it can lengthen his reach by hoisting him on the shoulders of his predecessors. Knowledge organized in a discipline does a good deal for the merely competent; it endows him with some effectiveness. It does infinitely more for the truly able; it endows him with excellence.

Executives have the economic job anyhow. Most work at it hard – too hard in many cases. This book poses no additional work. On the contrary, it aims to help them do their job with less effort and in less time, and yet with greater impact. It does not tell them how to do things right. It attempts to help them find the right things to do.

PART I

UNDERSTANDING
THE BUSINESS

1
Business Realities

That executives give neither sufficient time nor sufficient thought to the future is a universal complaint. Every executive voices it when he talks about his own working day and when he talks or writes to his associates. It is a recurrent theme in the articles and in the books on management.

It is a valid complaint. Executives should spend more time and thought on the future of their business. They also should spend more time and thought on a good many other things, their social and community responsibilities for instance. Both they and their businesses pay a stiff penalty for these neglects. And yet, to complain that executives spend so little time on the work of tomorrow is futile. The neglect of the future is only a symptom; the executive slights tomorrow because he cannot get ahead of today. That too is a symptom. The real disease is the absence of any foundation of knowledge and system for tackling the economic tasks in business.

Today's job takes all the executive's time, as a rule; yet it is seldom done well. Few managers are greatly impressed with their own performance in the immediate tasks. They feel themselves caught in a 'rat race', and managed by whatever the mailboy dumps into their 'in' tray. They know that crash programmes which attempt to 'solve' this or that particular 'urgent' problem rarely achieve right and lasting results. And yet, they rush from one crash programme to the next. Worse still, they know that the same problems recur again and again, no matter how many times they are 'solved'.

Before an executive can think of tackling the future, he must be able therefore to dispose of the challenges of today in less time and with greater impact and permanence. For this he needs a systematic approach to today's job.

There are three different dimensions to the economic task: (1) the present business must be made effective; (2) its potential must be identified and realized; (3) it must be made into a different business for a different future. Each task requires a distinct approach. Each asks different questions. Each comes out with different conclusions. Yet they are inseparable. All three have to be done at the same time: today. All three have to be carried out with the same organization, the same resources of men, knowledge and money, and in the same entrepreneurial process. The future is not going to be made tomorrow; it is being made today, and largely by the decisions and actions taken with respect to the tasks of today. Conversely, what is being done to bring about the future directly affects the present. The tasks overlap. They require one unified strategy. Otherwise, they cannot really get done at all.

To tackle any one of these jobs, let alone all three together, requires an understanding of the true realities of the business as an economic system, of its capacity for economic performance, and of the relationship between available resources and possible results. Otherwise, there is no alternative to the 'rat race'. This understanding never comes ready-made; it has to be developed separately for each business. Yet the assumptions and expectations that underlie it are largely common. Businesses are different, but business is much the same, regardless of size and structure, of products, technology and markets, of culture and managerial competence. There is a common business reality.

There are actually two sets of generalizations that apply to most businesses most of the time: one with respect to the results and resources of a business, one with respect to its efforts. Together they lead to a number of conclusions regarding the nature and direction of the entrepreneurial job.

Most of these assumptions will sound plausible, perhaps even familiar, to most businessmen, but few businessmen ever pull them together into a coherent whole. Few draw action conclusions from them, no matter how much each individual statement agrees with their experience and knowledge. As a result, few executives base their actions on these, their own assumptions and expectations.

1. *Neither results nor resources exist inside the business. Both exist outside.* There are no profit centres within the business; there are only cost centres. The only thing one can say with certainty about any business activity, whether engineering or selling, manufacturing or accounting, is that it consumes efforts and thereby incurs costs. Whether it contributes to results remains to be seen.

Results depend not on anybody within the business nor on anything within the control of the business. They depend on somebody outside – the customer in a market economy, the political authorities in a controlled economy. It is always some-body outside who decides whether the efforts of a business become economic results or whether they become so much waste and scrap.

The same is true of the one and only distinct resource of any business: knowledge. Other resources, money or physical equip-ment, for instance, do not confer any distinction. What does make a business distinct and what is its peculiar resource is its ability to use knowledge of all kinds – from scientific and technical know-ledge to social, economic and managerial knowledge. It is only in respect to knowledge that a business can be distinct, can therefore produce something that has a value in the market place.

Yet knowledge is not a business resource. It is a universal social resource. It cannot be kept a secret for any length of time. 'What one man has done, another man can always do again' is old and profound wisdom. The one decisive resource of business, therefore, is as much outside of the business as are business results.

Indeed, business can be defined as a process that converts an outside resource, namely knowledge, into outside results, namely economic values.

2. *Results are obtained by exploiting opportunities, not by solving problems.* All one can hope to get by solving a problem is to restore normality. All one can hope, at best, is to eliminate a restriction on the capacity of the business to obtain results. The results themselves must come from the exploitation of opportunities.

3. *Resources, to produce results, must be allocated to oppor-tunities* rather than to problems. Needless to say, one cannot shrug off all problems, but they can and and should be minimized

Economists talk a great deal about the maximization of profit in business. This, as countless critics have pointed out, is so vague a concept as to be meaningless. But 'maximization of opportunities' is a meaningful, indeed a precise, definition of the entrepreneurial job. It implies that effectiveness rather than efficiency is essential in business. The pertinent question is not how to do things right but how to find the right things to do, and to concentrate resources and efforts on them.

4. *Economic results are earned only by leadership,* not by mere competence. Profits are the rewards for making a unique, or at least a distinct, contribution in a meaningful area; and what is meaningful is decided by market and customer. Profit can only be earned by providing something the market accepts as value

and is willing to pay for as such. And value always implies the differentiation of leadership. The genuine monopoly, which is as mythical a beast as the unicorn (save for politically enforced, that is, governmental monopolies), is the one exception.

This does not mean that a business has to be the giant of its industry nor that it has to be first in every single product line, market, or technology in which it is engaged. To be big is not identical with leadership. In many industries the largest company is by no means the most profitable one, since it has to carry product lines, supply markets, or apply technologies where it cannot do a distinct, let alone a unique job. The second spot, or even the third spot is often preferable, for it may make possible that concentration on one segment of the market, on one class of customer, on one application of the technology, in which genuine leadership often lies. In fact, the belief of so many companies that they could – or should – have leadership in everything within their market or industry is a major obstacle to achieving it.

But a company which wants economic results has to have leadership in *something* of real value to a customer or market. It may be in one narrow but important aspect of the product line, it may be in its service, it may be in its distribution, or it may be in its ability to convert ideas into saleable products on the market speedily and at low cost.

Unless it has such leadership position, a business, a product, a service, becomes marginal. It may seem to be a leader, may supply a large share of the market, may have the full weight of momentum, history, and tradition behind it. But the marginal is incapable of survival in the long run, let alone of producing profits. It lives on borrowed time. It exists on sufferance and through the inertia of others. Sooner or later, whenever boom conditions abate, it will be squeezed out.

The leadership requirement has serious implications for business strategy. It makes most questionable, for instance, the common practice of trying to catch up with a competitor who has brought out a new or improved product. All one can hope to achieve thereby is to become a little less marginal. It also makes questionable 'defensive research' which throws scarce and expensive resources of knowledge into the usually futile task of slowing down the decline of a product that is already obsolete.

5. *Any leadership position is transitory and likely to be short-lived.* No business is ever secure in its leadership position. The market in which the results exist, and the knowledge which is the resource, are both generally accessible. No leadership position is more than a temporary advantage.* In business (as in a physical system) energy always tends towards diffusion. Business tends to drift from leadership to mediocrity. And the mediocre is three-quarters down the road to being marginal. Results always drift from earning a profit towards earning, at best, a fee which is all competence is worth.

It is, then, the executive's job to reverse the normal drift. It is his job to focus the business on opportunity and away from problems, to re-create leadership and counteract the trend towards mediocrity, to replace inertia and its momentum by new energy and new direction.

The second set of assumptions deals with the *efforts within the business and their cost.*

6. *What exists is getting old.* To say that most executives spend most of their time tackling the problems of today is euphemism. They spend most of their time on the problems of yesterday. Executives spend more of their time trying to unmake the past than on anything else.

This, to a large extent, is inevitable. What exists today is of necessity the product of yesterday. The business itself – its present resources, its efforts and their allocation, its organization as well as its products, its markets and its customers – expresses necessarily decisions and actions taken in the past. Its people, in the great majority, grew up in the business of yesterday. Their attitudes, expectations, and values were formed at an earlier time; and they tend to apply the lessons of the past to the present. Indeed, every business regards what happened in the past as normal, with a strong inclination to reject as abnormal whatever does not fit the pattern.

No matter how wise, forward-looking, or courageous the decisions and actions were when first made, they will have been overtaken by events by the time they become normal behaviour and the routine of a business. No matter how appropriate the

---

* This is nothing but a restatement of Schumpeter's famous theorem that profits result only from the innovator's advantage and therefore disappear as soon as the innovation has become routine.

attitudes were when formed, by the time their holders have moved into senior, policy-making positions, the world that made them no longer exists. Events never happen as anticipated; the future is always different. Just as generals tend to prepare for the last war, businessmen always tend to react in terms of the last boom or of the last depression. What exists is therefore always ageing. Any human decision or action starts to get old the moment it has been made.

It is always futile to restore normality; 'normality' is only the reality of yesterday. The job is not to impose yesterday's normal on a changed today; but to change the business, its behaviour, its attitudes, its expectations – as well as its products, its markets, and its distributive channels – to fit the new realities.

7. *What exists is likely to be misallocated.* Business enterprise is not a phenomenon of nature but one of society. In a social situation, however, events are not distributed according to the 'normal distribution' of a natural universe (that is, they are not distributed according to the bell-shaped Gaussian curve). In a social situation a very small number of events *at one extreme* – the first 10 per cent to 20 per cent at most – account for 90 per cent of all results; whereas the great majority of events account for 10 per cent or so of the results. This is true in the market place: a handful of large customers out of many thousands produce the bulk of orders; a handful of products out of hundreds of items in the line produce the bulk of the volume; and so on. It is true of sales efforts: a few salesmen out of several hundred always produce two-thirds of all new business. It is true in the plant: a handful of production runs account for most of the tonnage. It is true of research: the same few men in the laboratory are apt to produce nearly all the important innovations.

It also holds true for practically all personnel problems: the bulk of the grievances always comes from a few places or from one group of employees (for example, from the older unmarried women or from the clean-up men on the night shift), as does the great bulk of absenteeism, of turnover, of suggestions under a suggestion system, of accidents. As studies at the New York Telephone Company have shown, this is true even in respect of sickness.

The implications of this simple statement about normal distribution are broad.

It means, first: while 90 per cent of the results are being produced by the first 10 per cent of events, 90 per cent of the costs are incurred by the remaining and resultless 90 per cent of events. In other words, results and costs stand in inverse relationship to each other. Economic results are, by and large, directly proportionate to revenue, while costs are directly proportionate to the number of transactions. (The only exceptions are the purchased materials and parts that go directly into the final product.)

A second implication is that resources and efforts will normally allocate themselves to the 90 per cent of events that produce practically no results. They will allocate themselves to the number of events rather than to the results. In fact, the most expensive and potentially most productive resources (i.e., highly trained people) will misallocate themselves the worst. For the pressure exerted by the bulk of transactions is fortified by the individual's pride in doing the difficult – whether productive or not. This has been proved by every study. Let me give some examples:

A large engineering company prided itself on the high quality and reputation of its technical service group, which contained several hundred expensive men. The men were indeed first-rate. But analysis of their allocation showed clearly that while they worked hard, they contributed little. Most of them worked on the 'interesting' problems – especially those of the very small customers – problems which, even if solved, produced little business. The automobile industry was the company's major customer and accounted for almost one-third of all purchases. But few technical service people had within memory set foot in the engineering department or the plant of an automobile company. 'General Motors and Ford don't need me; they have their own people' was their reaction.

Similarly, in many companies, salesmen are misallocated. The largest group of salesmen (and the most effective ones) are usually put on the products that are hard to sell, either because they are yesterday's products or because they are also-rans which managerial vanity desperately is trying to make into winners. Tomorrow's important products rarely get the sales effort required. And the product that has sensational success in the market, and which therefore ought to be pushed all out, tends to be slighted. 'It is doing all right without extra effort, after all' is the common conclusion.

Research departments, design staffs, market development

efforts, even advertising efforts have been shown to be allocated the same way in many companies – by transactions rather than by results, by what is difficult rather than by what is productive, by yesterday's problems rather than by today's and to-morrow's opportunities.

A third and important implication is that revenue money and cost money are rarely the same money stream. Most businessmen see in their mind's eye – and most accounting presentations assume – that the revenue stream feeds back into the cost stream, which then, in turn, feeds back into the revenue stream. But the loop is not a closed one. Revenue obviously produces the wherewithal for the costs. But unless management constantly works at directing efforts into revenue-producing activities, the costs will tend to allocate themselves by drifting into nothing-producing activities, into sheer busy-ness.

In respect then to efforts and costs as well as to resources and results the business tends to drift towards diffusion of energy.

There is thus need for constant reappraisal and redirection; and the need is greatest where it is least expected: *in making the present business effective*. It is the present in which a business first has to perform with effectiveness. It is the present where both the keenest analysis and the greatest energy are required. Yet it is dangerously tempting to keep on patching yesterday's garment rather than work on designing tomorrow's pattern.

A piecemeal approach will not suffice. To have a real under-standing of the business, the executive must be able to see it in its entirety. He must be able to see its resources and efforts as a whole and to see their allocation to products and services, to markets, customers, end-uses, to distributive channels. He must be able to see which efforts go onto problems and which onto opportunities. He must be able to weigh alternatives of direction and allocation. Partial analysis is likely to misinform and misdirect. Only the over-all view of the entire business as an economic system can give real knowledge.

8. *Concentration is the key to real economic results.* Economic results require that managers concentrate their efforts on the smallest number of products, product lines, services, customers, markets, distributive channels, end-uses, and so on, that will produce the largest amount of revenue. Managers must minimize the amount of attention devoted to products which produce primarily costs

because, for instance, their volume is too small or too splintered.

Economic results require that staff efforts be concentrated on the few activities that are capable of producing significant business results.

Effective cost control requires a similar concentration of work and efforts on those few areas where improvement in cost performance will have significant impact on business performance and results – that is, on those areas where a relatively minor increase in efficiency will produce a major increase in economic effectiveness.

Finally, human resources must be concentrated on a few major opportunities. This is particularly true for the high-grade human resources through which knowledge becomes effective in work. And above all it is true for the scarcest, most expensive, but also potentially most effective of all human resources in a business: managerial talent.

No other principle of effectiveness is violated as constantly today as the basic principle of concentration. This, of course, is true not only of businesses. Governments try to do a little of everything. Today's big university (especially in the United States) tries to be all things to all men, combining teaching and research, community services, consulting activities, and so on. But business – especially large business – is no less diffuse.

Only a few years ago it was fashionable to attack American industry for 'planned obsolescence'. And it has long been a favourite criticism of industry, especially American industry, that it imposes 'deadening standardization'. Unfortunately industry is being attacked for doing what it should be doing and fails to do.

Large United States corporations pride themselves on being willing and able to supply any specialty, to satisfy any demand for variety, even to stimulate such demands. Any number of businesses boast that they never of their own free will abandon a product. As a result, most large companies end up with thousands of items in their product line – and all too frequently fewer than twenty really sell. However, these twenty or fewer items have to contribute revenues to carry the costs of the 9,999 non-sellers.

Indeed, the basic problem of United States competitive strength in the world today may be product clutter. If properly costed, the main lines in most of our industries prove to be fully competitive, despite our high wage rate and our high tax burden. But we fritter away our competitive advantage in the volume products by subsidizing an enormous array of specialties, of which only a few recover their true cost. In electronics, for instance, the competition of the Japanese portable transistor radio rests on little more than the Japanese concentration on a few models in this one line – as against the uncontrolled plethora of barely differentiated models in the United States manufacturers' lines.

We are similarly profligate in this country with respect to staff activities. Our motto seems to be: 'Let's do a little bit of everything' – personnel research, advanced engineering, customer analysis, international economics, operations research, public relations, and so on. As a result, we build enormous staffs, and yet do not concentrate enough effort in any one area.

Similarly, in our attempts to control costs, we scatter our efforts rather than concentrate them where the costs are. Typically the cost-reduction programme aims at cutting a little bit – say, 5 or 10 per cent – off everything. This across-the-board cut is at best ineffectual; at worst, it is apt to cripple the important, result-producing efforts which usually get less money than they need to begin with. But efforts that are sheer waste are barely touched by the typical cost-reduction programme; for typically they start out with a generous budget.

These are the business realities, the assumptions that are likely to be found valid by most businesses at most times, the concepts with which the approach to the entrepreneurial task has to begin. They have only been sketched here in outline; each will be discussed in detail in the course of the book.

That these are only assumptions should be stressed. They must be tested by actual analysis; and one or the other assumption may well be found not to apply to any one particular business at any one particular time. Yet they have sufficient probability to provide the foundation for the analysis the executive needs to understand his business. They are the starting points for the analysis needed for all three of the entrepreneurial tasks: making effective the present business; finding business potential; and making the future of the business.

The small and apparently simple business needs this understanding just as much as does the big and highly complex company. Understanding is needed as much for the immediate task of effectiveness today as it is for work on the future, many years hence. It is a necessary tool for any executive who takes seriously his entrepreneurial responsibility. And it is a tool which can neither be fashioned for him nor wielded for him. He must take part in making it and using it. The ability to design and develop this tool and the competence to use it should be standard equipment for the business executive.

2

The Result Areas

The basic business analysis starts with an examination of the business as it is now, the business as it has been bequeathed to us by the decisions, actions and results of the past. We need to see the hard skeleton, the basic stuff that is the economic structure. We need to see the relationship and intereactions of resources and results, of efforts and achievements, of revenues and costs.

Specifically we need first to identify and understand those areas in a business for which results can be measured. We can term these *result areas*. They are the businesses within the larger business complex; products and product lines (or service); markets (including customers and end-users); and distributive channels. This task is described in this chapter.

Chapter 3 relates result areas to the *revenue contributions* they make and to the *share of the cost burden* they generate. It analyses the *leadership position* and the *prospects* of each *result area*, and looks at the allocation to each of *key resources* such as knowledge-people and money. Chapter 4 leads up to a *tentative diagnosis* of result areas. Chapter 5, finally, subjects the *cost stream* to a similar analysis.

This analysis is in part a matter of 'getting the facts'. But even the first job, identifying result areas, requires business judgement. It requires decisions regarding the basic economic structure of the business which the 'facts', no matter how copious or how accurate, do not yield. Moreover, it requires decisions of considerable risk, decisions that will – and should – upset a good many people, should go against their ingrained habits, should provoke lively discussion and dissent.

These disagreements are important. They bring out searching questions about the company, its products, policies, direction, in the minds of the people who are closest to what really goes on. The questioners may, of course, misinterpret what they experience – but the experiences are none the less real and relevant. On matters of such importance disagreements should not be concealed or explained away. Nothing is more dangerous in questions of importance and impact than decision by acclamation. It is bound to be the wrong decision on the wrong problem.

The accent in this phase of the work should therefore be on

BOX I

The kind of analysis described here can be done quickly by a small crew. In a medium-sized company one member of the top management group took six months with the help of three or four bright young men borrowed from the main departments. The only figures used were accounting data and generally available economic and industry statistics. For everything else, especially for judgements such as the prospects for a product line, he asked the company's executives for their opinions. In some areas a small sample study was made. To test the leadership position of one product, for instance, one team member talked to some twenty salesmen and two dozen distributors, and had an outside firm run a small consumer survey. Every three weeks the whole team reported in full detail to top management and all department heads. Half a dozen questions required more time than the six months set aside originally. Two of them involved substantial outside efforts: a study of distributive-channel changes (which required bringing in a consulting firm to do an operations research job including a good deal of large-computer work); and a study of foreign markets, their trends, buying behaviour, and distribution systems. These, however, did not hold up the main decisions which were all in effect within a year after the study team first went to work. The executive in charge of the study was promoted to senior vice-president to work exclusively on the company's entrepreneurial development; his staff is kept small – never more than four or five young men brought in from the main departments on a rotating three- to five-year assignment.

Incidentally, this is no longer a 'medium-sized' but a pretty large company.

---

bringing out areas of disagreement and judgement rather than on achieving technical perfection in the analysis. What needs to be brought out is not 'right answers' but 'right questions'.

This does not mean that highly advanced tools and techniques – operations research or market analysis, advanced accounting systems or complex computer programmes – may not be needed even at this first stage, if the business is complex enough to require them and experienced enough to use them. But as a rule there is in this analysis an inverse relationship between usefulness of results and sophistication of tools and techniques. One should always ask: What is the *simplest* method that will give us adequate results? And what are the simplest tools? Albert Einstein after all never used anything more complicated than a blackboard.

Altogether in any analysis in which the results are likely to be the subject of hot discussion and strong opinions the accent should be on utmost simplicity of tools and techniques. Otherwise the unwelcome result will be smothered under long, pseudo-learnéd, discussion of the techniques. Or it will be brushed aside because the audience distrusts a complicated and mysterious method and suspects it – often rightly – of being a smoke screen for ignorance and intellectual arrogance.

The people in charge of this analysis should therefore be told to bring to top management the *uncertainties*, the ambiguities, the disagreements among themselves and within the senior management group before they even start on tentative conclusions. Only top management can really decide in these matters; for none of these decisions is a decision on 'facts' but on the business itself and its future courses of action.

DEFINING THE PRODUCT

The analysis of the result areas has to start with products (or services) and in particular with a definition of 'product'. Questions regarding product-definition, while not simple, are at least known and understood by every experienced executive. This alone makes product analysis the best place to start.

Practically every business has some 'products' which are not truly products at all but parts of some other product, an accessory or a sales promotion. To judge these by the standards of products is misleading. They ought to be judged by their contribution to the real products – by their capacity to promote sales, for instance. Conversely, a business may consider as sales promotion or as an accessory – that is, as 'part of the package' – what in reality is *the* product, if only because the rest of the package is not being bought.

The classic example of an apparent product that actually created the sales, is the Gillette safety razor, which was practically given away in large quantities so as to create a market for the very profitable razor blades. To expect a high return from the safety razor would have missed the point. The question to ask of such a product is not what it produces itself but whether it actually creates a market for the razor blades – and whether these then produce the economic results.

The experience of a manufacturer of office reproduction equipment was just the opposite. His 'safety razor' was the reproduction machine itself. His 'razor blades' were the supplies, the inks, the special stencils, the cleaning fluid, and so on, needed to obtain copies from the machine. The machine did well in the market. But the supply business, analysis showed, was not generated – it went to independent stationery suppliers that had better products and offered them at a lower price. The fact that the reproduction equipment did quite well was therefore irrelevant. It was not a 'product'. Its own success was actually failure in terms of the true products for which it was supposed to make the market. But the reproduction equipment turned out to be capable of being a very successful product indeed. Its sales went up sharply – even though the price was almost doubled – as soon as promotion for the equipment stopped harping on the need to use with it the company's own (inferior but expensive) supplies. As so often happens the customer was a better economist than the maker; for over the lifetime of such a machine much more is spent on the supplies than on the original equipment.

These are important business problems rather than questions of semantics. How management answers them determines what course of action it will choose.

Product A in a consumer-goods manufacturer's line is defined differently by each of the three members of top management. It sells in large quantities but it is extremely seasonal. It is a distinct product in its end-uses, its composition, its brand name and promotion, its costs and its price. But most of it – perhaps four-fifths – is not bought as a separate purchase but

through a combination offer in which product A and another –
and far less seasonal – product (B) are made available for about
three-quarters of what the two would cost if bought separately.
However this over-all price is advertised as being the full price
for A, plus half-price for B.

To the financial man therefore, A is not only a separate product but the company's best product. In his books it shows a
very high profit margin – for there the entire price reduction of
the combination offer is being charged to B. As a result he
wants to push A, make more of it, spend a larger share of
the promotion dollar on it, and so forth. And the company's
retailers agree with him.

For the manufacturing manager, however, A is not a 'product' at all. It is a premium offered to create demand for B at a
time when sales otherwise would be low. To him the main
result of the seasonal product A is to make possible steady
year-round output and much lower the cost of standard
product B (which, by the way, was the original purpose in
developing A). What he wants is to produce less of A but to
use it to move more of B. He therefore favours a lower list
price for A to make possible combination with a larger quantity of B. And he would only promote B.

The marketing executive, finally, considers the combination
to be the only 'product' – but a real and highly distinct one.
He wants to promote the combination as such, but he worries
because he considers the combined profit margin to be quite
low. And to protect the market standing of B he wants to
distribute the price reduction of the combination offer equally
between the two – which, for different reasons, both his
colleagues oppose.

Even Solomon could not decide which of the three is right.
Yet the company has to move one way or the other. Similar conun-
drums are presented whenever a whole host of products – each
with its own end-use and market – come inexorably out of one
process. Are the by-products of petroleum refining – that is, all
the scores of raw materials for plastics, insecticides, pharma-
ceuticals, dyestuffs – all *one* product? They are being produced,
by necessity almost, whenever crude oil is refined. What they are
and how much of each is turned out is largely determined by
what is in the crude oil rather than by what the refiners want to get.

Or what about the starches, adhesives, and oils that emerge whenever corn is industrially processed?

Or, on a much simpler level, are the various sizes, shapes,
colours in which an object may be sold all *one* product or many
products within one product line? Marketing logic usually gives
one answer, manufacturing logic another – and financial analysis
often still another.

THE THREE DIMENSIONS OF BUSINESS RESULTS

That a business gets paid for its products is so obvious that it is
never forgotten. But, though equally obvious, it is often overlooked that there has to be a market for the product. There also
have to be distributive channels to get the product from the producer to the market. But many businessmen – especially makers
of industrial products – are as unaware that they use distributive
channels, let alone that they depend on them, as Molière's M.
Jourdain was of the fact that he spoke prose.

Each of these three areas is only one dimension of result-producing activity, one result area. To each correspond specific
revenue contributions but also a specific share of the cost burden;
to each are committed specific resources; each has its own prospects;
and in each a position of leadership is needed.

But the three must also be analysed together and in their inter-
relationship. Indeed one of the most common causes of poor
performance is imbalance between the three. A product may do
poorly – to the point where it is about to be dropped. Yet it may
well be as good a product as its makers thought when they first
brought it out – but offered to the wrong market or through the
wrong distributive channel.

One of the largest American producers of packaged foods
brought out several years ago a line of gourmet foods. Whereas
all its other products were distributed through mass-retailers
of food, especially the supermarkets, the company decided to
distribute the gourmet foods through specialty stores only. The
line failed. Yet similar lines, offered a little later by much less
well-known companies through the supermarkets, did well. The
idea behind the gourmet foods was to offer the housewife the
opportunity to produce without any cooking skill an unusual
dinner once in a while. But for most housewives the food

specialty store is not an available distributive channel; they hardly know of its existence and certainly do not shop there. For those few who go in for elaborate cooking and shop in the specialty stores, processed and packaged food made by a mass-producer of staples is the wrong product, no matter what it is called.

The present predicament of the mass-circulation magazine in America is also in large measure a distributive channel problem. Mass-magazines selling many millions of copies a week, do not use mass-distribution. They solicit individual subscriptions and mail individual copies. The cost of obtaining and supplying one reader is substantially higher than the price that could possibly be charged for subscription. As a result, the advertiser pays for both the value he gets and the value the reader gets – and this he is understandably not eager to do. This explains why several famous magazines of yesterday went out of business just when they broke all circulation records.

For the American mass-circulation magazine to survive, it will have to find new channels of mass-distribution which combine bulk-subscription and bulk-transportation with delivery to the home. No such system is available today. That it is, however, not altogether inconceivable is shown by the example of the telephone; the costs are largely the costs of a mass-system while the service is in and through individual units.

Both the market and the distributive channel are often more crucial than the product. Products are within the business as the accountant defines it; they are within its legal boundaries. Economically the other two areas are as much part of the business. Indeed a product does not exist, economically speaking, except within a market, bought by a customer for an end-use, and brought to him through a distributive channel. Markets as well as distributive channels do exist, however, independently of any one product. They are primary; the product is secondary.

The two 'outside' areas are however much more difficult to control, precisely because they are outside. Management can order a product modification; it cannot order a market modification or a modification of distributive channels. These can be changed, to be sure, but only within narrow limits.

A manufacturer of branded and packaged products for application in the home firmly believed that only the specialized store – especially the furniture store – could give the service his products needed to do their job for the home owner. The products were excellent and had high consumer acceptance. They were well promoted. And the stores that carried them used well-trained sales people and were amply supplied with literature, displays and other sales supports. Yet sales were small and did not grow. The furniture store was simply the wrong channel for a nationally advertised, packaged product designed to be used every other month or so. Such a product is for mass-consumption and must be sold where mass-buying exists – and through distributors who, unlike furniture stores, want mass-buyers and are geared to them.

The manufacturer's strenuous attempts to get furniture stores to reach for mass-customers, and to get mass-customers to come to a specialty store for his products, led nowhere. In the end he had to accept the fact that in the American market of today, mass-distribution takes place where the masses shop; in supermarket, department store, shopping centre, and discount house. He had therefore to re-engineer his products by putting the needed service inside the package, that is, into the products. Only then did he get the benefit of his product quality, his customer acceptance, and his promotion – through mass-buying at the mass-distributors.

In respect to distributive channels there is one more complication which makes this a difficult as well as a crucial result area. There is no distributive channel which is not, at the same time, also a customer. As a distributive channel it must 'fit' the product on the one hand, and the market, customer, and end-use on the other hand. But the product in turn must be right for the distinct and important customer who serves as its distributive channel. If it is the wrong channel for the product or for the market, there will be failure. The product will not get to its market, will not be bought, will not produce results. But if it is the wrong product – or if it uses the wrong policies – the distributive channel, acting as a customer, will not buy.

Manufacturers of branded, mass-consumer goods are usually aware of this. At least they know they have two distinct customers, housewife and retailer, with different – and often conflicting – expectations and wants. But few others seem to know it.

Consumer-goods manufacturers typically see the retailer as the distributive channel, rather than as the customer. This, by the way, explains why dealer relations problems are chronic in industries such as home appliances.

Industrial-goods manufacturers, on the other hand, often miss the point that their customer is also their distributive channel. They see the paper industry or the bakeries, for example, as their market. But the industrial user also gets the electrical motor, the adhesive for paper, or the sweetening for bakery products to a market or customer and, above all, an end-use. If I make a chemical used solely in one stage of steel-making, my sales are ultimately dependent on the sales of steel. I can go out of business because the steel companies buy from someone else or use a different chemical; I can go out of business, in other words, because I lose the steel industry as a customer. But I shall also go out of business if the steel industry loses its market, no matter how much the steel companies like my product. If that happens I am out of business because I have lost my distributive channel.

The customer of an industrial-goods producer therefore plays a twofold role: he is genuine customer and genuine distributive channel. In either role he is crucial to the producer. And if the product does not disappear in the customers' manufacturing process (e.g. synthetic fibres used in cloth and garments), the producer had better concern himself also with what his industrial customers do for the final consumers' acceptance of his products.

Finally, in a modern economy, whether developed or developing, distributive channels change rapidly – more rapidly, as a rule, than either technology or customer expectations and values. Indeed I have never seen a decision with respect to distributive channels that was not obsolescent five years later, and badly in need of new thinking and fundamental change.

Markets as well as distributive channels deserve a good deal of attention and study – much more than they usually receive. Their analysis is likely to turn up more new insights and more opportunities (but also more unpleasant surprises) than the analysis of the product area. But the burden of pushing through the step-by-step process of analysis, of establishing its purposes and its concepts, and of proving its diagnostic power must rest on the analysis of the product as the most familiar and easiest of the result areas.*

* This is not necessarily true for a department store where typical customer purchase may be a better starting point; at least the customary analysis by the

There is only one major exception to this rule. Wherever genuine businesses exist within a larger business complex, they should be the starting point. They are not only a bigger unit than a product or a product line (or a service). Their results are more nearly 'real', and so are their resources – both because they are usually distinct and separate, and because the capital investment in such a business is usually known within a fairly narrow range; while capital invested in one of many products within a business cannot generally even be surmised. Responsibility for a business within a business can be established and goals can be set. These are of course all arguments in favour of decentralization, and when it comes to analysis of a business, they are telling arguments indeed. But after the analysis of a whole such business, its main result areas have to be analysed one by one – and then together. And this starts us off again on an analysis of the products, though on a higher level of insight and understanding.

---

usual departments and their products is not too revealing. And an American commercial bank may also find the customer a better foundation for analysis than the various services of different departments; our commercial banks are, after all, financial supermarkets.

3

Revenues, Resources and Prospects

What are the essentials, the few but fundamental facts on which
to base a diagnosis of a business and its result areas? Every executive
today is inundated with figures. And more and more data pour out
every day. Which ones really have something to say? And how
do they have to be presented to convey meaning rapidly, effectively,
reliably?

What one might call a 'Business X-ray' is the subject of this
and the following chapters. These chapters deal with concepts.
They present ideas, however, through a concrete illustration: a
presentation – though grossly simplified – of an actual analysis of
an existing business (which I shall call Universal Products). It
is a middle-sized, reasonably prosperous manufacturing company,
differing from many others of the same kind only in having been
for decades equally active in the American and European markets,
with plants, sales forces and managements on both sides of the
Atlantic.

Only one result area is actually presented in the analysis: products. But the same concepts apply to the analyses of the other
result areas – customers, markets, end-uses and distributive
channels. Nor does it make much difference whether a business
makes a physical product or renders a service.

This form of analysis examines the *entire product range of a
business* rather than one product at a time. All the data relate the
performance, costs, resources and prospects of an individual product to over-all business results and over-all business resources
and efforts.

The analysis uses mostly normal accounting data – except, for
the concept of 'transactions' which is explained on page 31. The
form in which these data are presented (see Table I) may, however,
seem unfamiliar (though executives who have used break-even
point analyses and financial analyses will recognize old acquaint-
ances*).

* Of the large and growing literature on these two analytical techniques the
American books I have found of greatest value – both in explaining concepts and
in developing techniques for the businessman – are Rautenstrauch & Villiers, *The*

TABLE I

UNIVERSAL PRODUCTS COMPANY:

A SCHEMATIC EXAMPLE OF PRODUCT ANALYSIS

(dollars in millions)

Total company sales	$145			
Purchased raw materials	50			
Fixed charges	15			
	——	Net profit before taxes		$14.5
Available product revenues	$ 80	Costs assignable to products		65.5

Prod-uct	Revenue		Share in Cost Burden		Net Revenue Contribution		Contribution Coefficient[a]
	Value	*Percentage of Company Total*	Value	*Percentage of Company Total*	Value	*Percentage of Net Profit*	
A	$19.0	24.0%	$18.2	28.0%	$0.72	5.0%	0.26%
B	14.0	17.5	16.7	25.5	−2.7	−12.0	Loss
C	14.0	17.5	7.2	11.0	6.8	47.0	3.3
D	11.0	14.0	5.2	7.5	5.8	40.0	3.8
E	7.0	9.0	5.4	8.0	1.6	11.0	1.5
F	4.0	5.0	3.4	5.0	0.6	4.0	1.0
G	4.0	5.0	3.6	5.5	0.45	3.0	0.75
H	3.5	4.5	3.3	5.0	0.2	1.5	0.5
I	2.0	2.5	1.85	2.5	0.15	1.0	0.5
J	Under 1.0	1.0	1.5	2.0	−0.5	−0.5	Loss

[a] Obtained by dividing the net revenue contribution as a percentage of net profit before taxes (preceding column) by the value of the product revenue (first column).

Economics of Industrial Management, 2nd ed. (New York: Funk & Wagnalls, 1957) – especially on break-even points; and Joel Dean, *Managerial Economics* (Englewood Cliffs, N.J.: Prentice Hall, 1951) – especially for financial analysis. Many of the newer publications use far more advanced techniques, especially of a mathematical nature. There are situations where the advanced techniques are of material help, e.g., for the analysis of product-mix and product-time problems in a continuous materials stream such as that of a petroleum refinery. Much more advanced methods are also required for systems analysis, for instance in a major space vehicle development programme. But in most business situations cruder, less complex methods are good enough; the refinements now available may improve results in these situations but do not fundamentally change them.

The starting point of our analysis is the 'Business Realities' described in Chapter 1.

> Revenue money and cost money are not necessarily one stream.
>
> Business phenomena follow the normal distribution of social events in which 90 per cent of effects follow from the first 10 per cent of the causes and vice versa.
>
> Revenues are therefore proportionate to volume, with the bulk of the volume and of the corresponding revenues produced by a small fraction of the product numbers (markets, customers, etc.).
>
> Costs are therefore proportionate to transactions, with the bulk of the costs attributable to the large number – 90 per cent perhaps – of the transactions that produce only a small fraction of revenues.

WHY NOT USE COST ACCOUNTING?

That costs are, on the whole, directly proportionate to transactions should occasion little surprise. For example:

> To get a $50,000 order costs no more, as a rule, than to get a $500 order; certainly it does not cost 100 times as much.
>
> To design a new product that does not sell is as expensive as to design a winner.
>
> It costs just as much to do the paper work for a small order as for a large one – the same order entry, production order, scheduling, billing, collecting and so on.
>
> It even costs almost as many dollars to turn out the product for a small order as for a large one, to manufacture it, package it, store and ship it. For the only thing that may take less time in the small order is the actual manufacturing; and that is, as a rule, a subordinate cost factor in today's industry. Everything else takes as much time and handling.

Still, many businessmen will ask, why not base our analysis on cost accounting? It tells us, doesn't it, what the precise costs are? The answer is that it is misuse of cost accounting to derive from it figures for a particular product's share of total business costs.

> Cost accounting has to find a place for every penny spent. Where the cost accountant cannot document what costs are directly incurred in making this or that product, he must

therefore allocate. He can only do so by assuming that all non-direct costs are distributed either in proportion to direct costs or in proportion to the sales price of a product. This is all right as long as allocation is confined to a small margin of all costs – say, 10 or 20 per cent. In the production situation of fifty years ago this was the case. Today, however, the large majority of all costs are not direct; that is, are not incurred when and only when one unit of a certain product is being made. Only raw materials and supplies bought on the outside can still be considered truly direct costs. Even so-called 'direct labour' does not today fluctuate with unit volume of output. It remains pretty much unchanged whatever mix of products goes through a plant. Most of it even remains unchanged regardless of total output. Labour in most manufacturing, and in all service, industries is a charge related to time rather than to volume of output or to units of a product. Altogether less than a quarter of all costs, other than purchased raw materials, can in modern business be treated as truly direct; that is, as truly varying with, and dependent on, a given unit of a given product or process.

For the cost accountant's purposes this may matter little. Allocating costs in fixed proportion to the volume or price of a product may not materially distort the relationship between the various cost elements that make up the total unit cost of a product, for instance the relation between its fabricating costs and its finishing costs. Cost figures, in other words, still show, with reliability, where cost relations are out of line. But for the purpose of knowing what it costs a business to carry this or that product, figures that allocate the great bulk of the cost are useless. They prejudge what they are meant to document – namely, how the cost burden is distributed. Moreover, they make the one assumption least likely to be correct: that costs are distributed in a 'normal' Gaussian bell-shaped curve, that is, in proportion to results.

There are exceptions: for instance, a business that has, essentially, only one product.

General Motors, with the bulk of its output in one product family – automobiles – has been using for forty years a cost concept which assumes that each car bears a share of the cost burden equal to the total costs of the plant when running at

80 per cent of capacity, divided by the number of cars it would produce at 80 per cent capacity. This too is generalization and has only probability; but it is a simpler generalization than ours though it expresses a similar cost definition.

And where there are very large and distinct individual cost centres, such as ships in the fleet of a steamship line or jet planes of an airline, actual costs can be known and used. But otherwise actual costs cannot, as a rule, be extracted. Their behaviour has to be assumed.

Distribution according to transactions is the only close approximation to the behaviour of the costs of work not focused on, and carried by, an identifiable unit of production. The bulk of all costs in business today is of this kind.

The single major cost category that is usually clearly identifiable with respect to a specific product is irrelevant both to the revenue contribution and to the share of the cost burden. This is the cost for purchased raw materials and parts. A simple example – taken from a company making small electrical household appliances such as toasters, coffee makers, and flat irons – will illustrate this:

Purchased materials and parts account for 60 per cent of the manufacturer's price in the case of product A, for 30 per cent in the case of product B. Both sell the same volume. Profit margin is 10 per cent of manufacturer's price for both products. Both, therefore, are believed to do equally well. But actually the manufacturer makes one dollar in profits for any three dollars worth of his own resources and efforts invested in product A; he has to spend six dollars worth of his own resources and efforts to make one dollar on product B. If both products had a ready market for a larger output at the same price, though the manufacturer had resources to expand only one—

He would get twice as much additional output by putting his resources into product A rather than into product B. An additional unit of product A requires only thirty dollars worth of resources against a requirement of sixty dollars for product B.

He would therefore get twice as much profit through expanding product A rather than product B.

Both revenue contribution and cost burden share therefore

should use a 'value-added' figure* in which purchased materials and parts have been subtracted from the totals of sales and costs.

The conventional profit margin is also only one factor in the profit stream, which is profit margin multiplied by turnover. Two products, each selling for $10.00, may have the same raw-materials content and the same profit margin of $1.50 per unit. But if five units of one are made and sold while only one unit of the other is sold, the first will yield five times the profit dollars of the other. This is elementary; but businessmen tend to forget it, unless the figures they use include both factors (as for instance, in the well-publicized return-on-investment figures of the DuPont Company). All concepts and figures used in the analysis here are therefore profit-stream figures, including both profit margins and turnover.

Those costs which are *independent* of any given volume of work and production should also be excluded from the basic calculation. These are the *truly* fixed costs – rent and property taxes, insurance, maintenance, and above all the costs of servicing capital that has already been invested and has therefore to be paid for, whatever the volume of sales or of profits (the costs commonly called 'sunk costs' by accountants and economists).† When fixed costs are very high they require a separate cost allocation – an illustration is given on pages 35–6 where the cost burden of freight on a steamship is being analysed.

We thus arrive at the following definitions:

Net sales are simply sales of the company less purchased raw materials.

Total company revenues are net sales minus fixed costs (some people call them '*disposable revenues*').

Revenue of a product is the percentage of *total company revenues* that corresponds to the percentage which sales of the product (minus the purchased raw materials and

* 'Value added in manufacturing' is the commonly used term. It would be much better to speak of 'cost added', whether in manufacturing or in distribution. In the first place only the customer adds value. All manufacturer and distributor can do is to add costs. Secondly, what one wants to find out is what part of this added cost is being turned into value and how much is friction and waste. But the term 'value added' is so generally accepted that it would be pedantry to change it.

† Whether 'profit', in so far as it corresponds to the minimum rate that has to be paid for capital on the market, is a 'sunk cost' need not concern us here – though it is an important question in business economics. As Box II on pages 32–3 shows, it is taken out of the figures anyhow.

supplies directly and uniquely attributable to the product) constitute of company net sales.

Share of the cost burden of a product is the percentage of *total company cost* (less purchased raw materials and fixed costs) that corresponds to the percentage share of the *transactions* attributable to the product in the total volume of such transactions in the business.

Net revenue contribution is, of course, nothing but the difference between *revenues* of a product and its *share of the cost* burden.*

Contribution coefficient – i.e., the ability of a product to generate revenue as its volume goes up or down – is the *net revenue contribution* of the product for each million dollars of sales. It can be expressed, of course, as a percentage of *total company revenues* per million dollar of sales of the product or as a dollar amount of additional sales needed to increase total *revenues* by a given percentage or by a given amount.† This is a measure of the results to be expected if volume of one product is substituted for volume of another product. In other words, *contribution coefficient* assumes that total volume remains the same. Even with this qualification it is only a rough approximation. It is close enough to serve as guide to the impact on over-all results that might ensue from attempts to push sales of any one of the products.

BUT WHAT IS A TRANSACTION?

The term used so far may sound strange; but the concepts they express are surely familiar.

There is one exception here, however, one new concept requiring data rarely produced by the accounting system: the *transaction*.

What is a transaction? Above all, how does one decide which

---

* *Net revenue contribution* approximates, as the illustration in Box II on pages 32–3 points out, profit or loss on a product only where fixed costs are a relatively small part of the total – below 20 per cent of total costs or so.

† Any business using such techniques as the multiple-product break-even analysis (see Rautenstrauch & Villiers, *op. cit.*), would of course take the figure for *contribution coefficient* from there. However, this is not a commonly used technique – though businessmen should understand it even if its complexity prevents their using it.

of the many transactions within a business is the transaction that is representative of the actual cost structure?

There is no set answer. The nature of the business determines this rather than accounting practices or economic theorems.

In many businesses the number of invoices sent out is the simplest and most easily obtainable unit of transaction. Where paper work with its heavy cost is organized around it, the individual invoice can be used with reasonable reliability as an index of the actual cost share of a product. Sometimes shipments are a more convenient unit, especially where there are many different products on one invoice.

In department stores, purchase per customer has long been known as a good indicator of cost structure. The larger the purchase per customer, the greater the effectiveness of the retail operation. The number of customers that have to come into the store to move a certain quantity of a certain item of merchandise may well be a more reliable unit of transactions for department stores than any other.

A medium-sized company that makes computers for scientific work uses, as unit of transactions, the number of proposals that have to be made to obtain one order. The proposal, with all the enormous technical and clerical work that accompanies it, is the true cost centre – and also the maw into which the scarcest and most expensive resources, the best technical talents of the company, disappear.

In an aluminium rolling-mill, the proper unit of transactions was found to be the number of production runs through the hot-rolling stage. In the extrusion plant of the same company, however (which makes products such as radiator grilles for automobiles or door handles for refrigerators), the appropriate unit of transaction was found to be the number of skilled die-makers'-hours needed to prepare the presses for any one specific shape.

For a commercial airline the most meaningful cost unit is the number of seat-miles available but not sold on a given route or a given flight, that is, a 'cost of not doing'. But for a consumer-goods company making goods distributed through many independent retailers, the right transaction unit may well be the number of calls on dealers for each million dollars sales of a product. It may even be the number of dealers needed to sell its volume. To service any dealer on the books costs pretty much the same – and it comes high. If there is any difference, it is in favour of the larger dealer who usually

BOX II

A sample calculation might help to show how these concepts can be used. It shows three different products – three different kinds of metal containers made in one can-making plant.

Total company sales amounted to $150 million. *Raw materials* purchased came to $50 million, leaving *net sales* of $100 million. *Total* fixed charges amounted to $30 million a year, leaving *total product revenues* of $70 million. Product X had sales of $40 million; its purchased raw-material content – somewhat lower than average – was $10 million, leaving *revenues* of $30 million or 30 per cent of *total company revenues*. Its *revenue* – 30 per cent of company sales minus raw materials, minus fixed charges – was thus figured at $21 million (30 per cent of $70 million).

Total company costs were $135 million. Minus *purchased raw materials* and minus *fixed charges*, this left $55 million as *total costs attributable to products*. The unit of *transaction* found to be most nearly representative was shipments – with a total of 250,000 a year. Of these product X accounted – as established by a sample study – for 60,000 or 24 per cent. This left it with a *share of the cost burden* of $13.2 million (24 per cent of $55 million), and with a *net revenue contribution* of $7.8 million (which, as will be seen, was more than half of the total company profit of $15 million ($150 million of sales less $135 million of costs). Its *contribution coefficient* would thus be $195,000 for each additional $1 million of sales.

(Continued next page)

requires fewer sales calls and less service – apart from being usually a better credit risk and paying more promptly.

For process industries with high capital investment, paper-

making for instance or petrochemicals, the most meaningful
unit for cost calculation may be time: the time it takes to get
out the same sales value (minus purchased materials, of course)

BOX II (*continued*)

Product Y accounted similarly for 22 per cent of *total revenues* –
with a *revenue* of $15.4 million. But it accounted for 30 per cent
of the transactions – or for a *share of the cost burden* of $16.5
million; and a *negative revenue contribution* of $1.1 million.
Product Z likewise showed a *negative revenue contribution* –
$3.4 million – with 18 per cent of *total revenue* ($12.6 million)
but with a 29 per cent *share in the total cost burden* ($16 million).
Fixed costs in this business are, however, rather high. And the
figures shown here are figures *after fixed-cost absorption*. This
means that each of the three products had already made its
contribution to fixed costs before the *net revenue contribution*
calculated here. Not producing products Y and Z would therefore be more costly than producing them without recovering
their total cost – which is, of course, what a *negative contribution*
means: if (a) their *negative contributions* are smaller than their
share of the *fixed costs*; and if (b) no other, better-yielding
product could be substituted for them in total production and
sales. (The latter is the crucial assumption. It is always implied
but is rarely tested. Therefore the fixed cost absorption argument
tends to become uncritical alibi in many cases.) As to the proportion of *fixed costs* chargeable to a product, one can use either
an amount proportionate to its *revenues* or one proportionate
to its *cost share*. I prefer the latter – not because it has a stronger
logical case, but because it is a more stringent test of the weaker
products. Under either method products Y and Z would be
found to have absorbed enough *fixed charges* to have added to
the *net profit* available to the company – though product Z is
marginal even by this test.

---

of different products. In such industries costs tend to be a
function of the hours run.

To determine which transaction is appropriate for a given
business is part of the analysis of the business. By itself it is a

big step towards understanding a business and its economics. It is also a genuine business decision of great impact – and of high risk. Analysts or technicians might point out the available choices and their consequences. The final decision is management's responsibility.

The power of the transactional analysis of business costs was recently demonstrated in a study of profits and costs of the grocery business conducted in 1963 by the New York management consulting firm McKinsey & Co. for the General Foods Corporation, America's largest producer of processed foods. Traditionally, the grocer – like most retailers – has charged an 'average' cost figure against a 'gross profit margin'. He has therefore considered that item to be the most profitable that gave the largest gross profit margin – though well-managed supermarket chains have increasingly taken speed of turnover into account as well. The McKinsey study showed, however, that actual costs depend on the transactions each commodity needs, and that the share of the cost burden of different commodities varies greatly. The profit margin of a case of dry cereal, for instance, is almost exactly the same as that of a case of canned soup: $1.26 for the cereal and $1.21 for the soup. The grocer therefore always considered the two commodities as producing the same profit for him. But the transactional study showed that the actual profit on the cereal is only 25 cents per case as against a profit of 71 cents for the soup. And even though baby foods both have a high gross margin and move fast, they require so much handling that they actually lose money for the grocer.

Managers may never have thought of their business as a 'transactional system'. But once they grasp the idea (especially if conveyed by examples rather than by learned dissertation), they can usually apply it to the business they know. At least the managers' intuition will point to the right answers.

Differences of opinion among experienced managers in a company are revealing and valuable. In a given business there may well be different transactions that could serve as the unit of cost. I know one large chemical company where invoices, number of service calls to help customers use a product, and product modifications for specific uses might each be claimed to be the representative unit of transactions and the true measurement of cost. If the cost picture of a product differs sharply as different yardsticks are used, this in itself is relevant information. At least it explains to the people in the business why there have been clashes of opinion regarding the merits and performance of the product in question.

In businesses where distinct and separate operations can be isolated, the cost for each operation, based on its typical transactions, can – and usually should – be determined. The costs of all operations added together give total cost burden.

This is the right procedure where operating costs are both high and virtually fixed. One cannot sail part of a ship; hence the total costs of sailing the entire ship are always incurred whether the ship is full or empty. Similarly, the pulp mill of a paper plant can either be run or it can be shut down; it cannot run at half-speed. Its operating costs are fixed, incurred in full whenever any pulp is being made, and also high.

To illustrate: Three distinct operations can be identified in any freight shipment by sea. There is a clerical operation which is geared to the number of separate shipments. Whether the shipment is large or small, valuable or low-cost, bulky or compact, twenty-five items on one invoice or one, the clerical cost is the same. It is fixed by law; the legally prescribed documents must be issued and handled. The clerical cost burden of any shipment is therefore the share of the total clerical costs divided by the total number of shipments for the shipping route served. Then there is the loading operation. Here the cost unit is the hour of loading and unloading time. The loading net can only make so many trips per hour, whether it carries a big load or a small one. And there always has to be a full loading crew in the ship's hold and on the pier. Time is the unit of cost. The loading-cost share is the total loading cost divided by a shipment's share of total loading time. This means, of course, that a large package is much more economical for the shipping line than a small one.

Finally, there are the costs of ship operations which are practically fixed whatever the ship carries. Capital costs, maintenance, crew wages, insurance – even fuel – are just as high when a ship sails empty as when it sails full. The ship-operations burden of a shipment is therefore that share of total ship-operations cost that corresponds to the percentage of the ship's loading space occupied by revenue freight on the typical voyage which a shipment occupies.

Total cost share of a shipment is the sum of these three separate cost shares.

The analysis so far will already have yielded important results. It will have brought out new facts and will have shed light on matters that had been troubling people in the business for a long time. It will have raised many new – and often disturbing – questions (especially when the result areas other than products are being analysed). In two places at least, important management decisions will have come to the surface: in the definition of a product and in defining the appropriate transaction unit.

We still, however, know too little about a product until its leadership position and its prospects – the outside and the future – have been looked at. Table II gives a sample.

WHAT MAKES FOR LEADERSHIP?

Experienced businessmen know that the seemingly simple statements regarding position and prospects of each product in Table II represent the final summation of a great deal of hard work and prolonged discussion. In these areas even calm men will get angry, and reasonable men will refuse to listen to facts with a curt: 'I don't believe it.' Here, in other words, is need for thorough, painstaking work. But the work itself – its tools and techniques, from value-analysis of the product to market research – is well known, has indeed been routine for years even in fairly small businesses. The results, in other words, may be controversial and hard to accept; but the work itself is familiar.

Of course, presentation in a large and complex company will be far more detailed than in smaller businesses. A good deal will be quantified, and so on. But it is not my intention here to show how complicated one can become – nor does anyone need this lesson. I am intent only on getting across a concept – and the concept *is* simple.

Leadership is not a quantitative term. The business with the largest share of a market may have leadership in one segment only. The monopolist, the single supplier of a product or of a market, never has leadership and cannot have it.

To have leadership a product must be best fitted for one – or

TABLE II

UNIVERSAL PRODUCTS COMPANY PRODUCT ANALYSIS: LEADERSHIP

(dollars in millions)

Product	Revenue	Leadership Position	Short-term Prospects Without Changes	With Changes	Static
A	$19.0	Marginal. As good as but no better than 3 or 4 other products on market. Tied for first place in sales.		Down	
B	14.0	Marginal. Is now 5 years old. Our entry in quality market. Sales should now be at least twice actual. Made several price cuts, but orders did not increase.	Down	Down?	x
C	14.0	Leader. Success surprised us. Introduced as premium product for small segment of market. Makes heavy inroads in regular market for A. Leads all others in ease of application.	Down	Up	
D	11.0	Leader. Low-priced line with unsatisfactory profit margins. Lacks quality of B but is being bought heavily by market B was designed for. Lasts almost twice as long as competitive models and costs 20% less than cheapest competitor.	Up	Strongly up	
E	7.0	Marginal. Distinct market—medium-sized business. Little growth. Customers prefer higher-priced product of competitor; claim ours gives trouble.	Down	Up	
F	4.0	Marginal, but leads in special market. Preferred for one specific industrial application. Bought because of service we give.			x
G	4.0	Similar to F. Same comments apply.	Up (limited)		
H	3.5	Marginal. Was expected to become company's major entry in new industrial market which has not developed so far. Competitor's process technically inferior but much cheaper.			x
I	2.0	Dead. Major product 10–15 years ago. Bought now for one obsolete process used in smaller companies only.			x
J	Under 1.0	Expected to be leader. Just brought out of development. Should enable customers to run their equipment much faster and for longer periods.	Up	Strongly up	

more – of the genuine wants of market and customer. It must be a genuine want. The customer must be willing to pay for it. No matter how desirable a certain quality in a product might appear to the manufacturer, it only gives leadership if the customer accepts the claim. His acceptance is his willingness to honour the claim in tangible form by preferring the product to its competitors – and by being willing to pay.

The monopolist cannot have leadership because the customer cannot choose. Customers of a monopoly always want a second supplier and flock to him when he appears. They may have been fully satisfied with the monopolist's goods or services. But it is an exceptional business or product that, after having had a monopoly, retains customer preference.*

The monopolist is therefore always in danger of becoming marginal the moment a second supplier appears. Most businessmen know this to be true – but emotionally they find it hard to accept. Yet, in analysing a business, one had best consider an unchallenged product as an endangered product.

The common test of leadership by 'share of the market' is also deceptive. Examples abound of companies that have the largest share of the market but are far behind in their profitability compared to competitors of much smaller apparent stature. This means that they do not get paid for leadership but, in effect, have to pay for it. For while the very large company has to be active in every area, no company, as a rule, can have real distinction in everything.

In all of American industry there is only one example of a

---

* Incidentally, the sole-source supplier has lower sales, as a rule, than he would have were there competitors in the field. Sales of a product line of any consequence do not begin to expand, let alone to reach their potential, as long as only one company supplies them. The history of the aluminium industry in the United States is an example. Though the Aluminum Company of America was the very model of the 'enlightened monopolist' who constantly lowers price and seeks new uses for his product, the explosive expansion of aluminium consumption in this country started after the United States government, during World War II, had put two other companies into the aluminium business. Part of the reason for this failure of monopoly to benefit even the monopolist is certainly that one company, no matter how big, is rarely big enough to develop a new market of any size by itself; it takes at least two. There is rarely 'one right way' in a new market. Yet alternatives are unlikely to be thought of or aggressively explored unless there is the challenge of competition. Another reason is probably that even the 'enlightened monopolist' tends to neglect markets and customers that cannot go elsewhere. But a main reason is certainly that manufacturer, wholesaler, retailer, or consumer dislikes to be dependent on a single source of supply and therefore keeps down his purchases from a supplier in control of the market.

company that combines first rank in every area with first rank in profitability in every area: General Motors in the U.S. automobile market. DuPont de Nemours, while the largest and most profitable of American chemical companies, works only in a few segments of industrial chemistry, especially in chemicals and fibres for the textile market. There are, to be sure, few situations comparable to that of U.S. Steel, the price and volume leader in most steel markets for many years but until a few years ago the least profitable large American steel company. Here, the largest share of the market seems to have been held by a producer who was marginal in the major product areas. But in most industries the largest company has leadership in only a few areas, while its very size and prominence force it to be active in a great many others.

Only an occasional very small specialty business can be the leader with all of its products or services, in all its markets and end-uses, with all its customers, and in all its distributive channels. But no company, no matter how large or how small, can afford to be marginal in all of them. Above all it cannot afford to be anything but a leader in the areas which are the mainstay of its business, produce the bulk of the sales, generate the bulk of the costs, and absorb the most important and most valuable resources. A marginal product generates inadequate returns. It is always in danger of being squeezed out altogether.

The larger the market the more dangerous is it to be marginal, the less room is there for any but products with genuine leadership position.

Contrary to what economists have been preaching for two hundred years, the alternative to monopoly in a developed, large market is not free competition – that is, an unlimited number of participants in an industry; but oligopoly – that is, competition between a fairly small number of manufacturers or suppliers. As the market gets bigger, it may take so much money to enter the industry that the attempt can be made only once in a great while – simply because one must either sell nationally or not sell at all (as in the American automobile industry). The bigger the market, the more will distributive channels concentrate on just enough well-known brands to give the customer meaningful choice, but not so many as to confuse him or as to require excessive inventories.

For this reason, for instance, concentration of the American kitchen-appliance industry (refrigerators, ranges, dishwashers, automatic laundries, etc.) on no more than half a dozen or so major brands will occur sooner or later whatever the anti-trust laws may say to the contrary. Five to six major brands are all that a large appliance dealer – whether a discount house, a department store, or a shopping centre – needs in order to have a full line which gives the customer all the selection he wants.

More brands, as a matter of fact, may only confuse the customer and may make him not want to buy. More brands do not increase sales, but they do increase inventory. They tie up money, floor space, and warehouse space. They make repair service difficult: the repairman has to be trained on more appliances and has to carry more spare parts. They either require additional promotion money or splinter the promotion impact, and so on. The first reaction of the appliance dealer in this situation is to put pressure for 'extras' on the manufacturers of the slower-selling lines. During the last decade dealers have asked for and received lower prices, larger discounts, special financing, extra promotion allowances, and guarantees of repurchase of used appliances at a stipulated price well above the market. Each demand meant a decrease in the manufacturer's profitability.

If and when a really sharp setback in the appliance market occurs, the marginal brands will then be squeezed out alto-gether – simply because dealers have to curtail their inventories and therefore concentrate on the few fast-selling brands and drop the others.

The main reason why concentration increases, the larger and more highly developed the market, is that the large market makes for meaningful product differentiation. The larger the market the less room it has for products that are 'just as good', the less room there is for marginal products and marginal producers.

This may be of particular importance today for Europe and for Japan where the mass-market is developing rapidly. A business or product that was a leader in the restricted German or French market of yesterday may rapidly become marginal in the mass-market of the unified European continent. This is certainly a major factor behind the rapid mergers and partnership associations between medium-sized companies – especially family-owned ones –

across Common Market national boundaries. And unless they try to establish monopolies that restrict the market, such combinations of medium-sized businesses into one large group or association are healthy – are indeed needed fully to exploit the economic potential of the Common Market or of Japan's new mass-consumer economy.

The expansion of a market also creates opportunities for a host of products and services with special characteristics to attain leadership position in a distinct market-segment or end-use which, while significantly smaller than the national or mass market, is still larger than what passed for the big market only a while back.

Take for example the market for specially formulated polymer petro-chemicals. The manufacturers of the large, volume polymer products – e.g., the main plastics – are the principal customers; and the opportunities, sales and profits for the accomplished polymer chemist are high. The Cummins Engine Company of Columbus, Indiana – a medium-sized business – has enjoyed highly profitable leadership as a maker of engines for heavy trucks. If the very large engineering companies (General Motors above all) did not offer a broad assortment of diesel engines for all uses – in buses, in ships, in locomotives – Cummins could hardly have confined itself to the specialization on one narrow line that underlies its success. Either an engine design is used widely or it becomes so difficult to instal and service that it is not used at all. Some small manufacturers, each specializing in one or two special applications of low-horse-power electrical motors, have been doing proportionately better than General Electric or Westinghouse, whose dominant market share forces them to supply all kinds of motors to all customers and for all end-uses, and who therefore, of necessity, must be marginal or lose money on some lines.

A leadership position may be based on price or on reliability. Easy maintenance may be crucial in one product for one purpose; a promise that no maintenance is needed may be leadership for a similar product in some other use (e.g., for a telephone cable laid on the ocean floor or for a microwave relay station for telephone and television signals built on a mountain top in Idaho, sixty miles and two blizzards from the nearest town). Appearance, style, design – customer recognition and acceptance – lowest cost of a finished article into which a product is being converted – small or large size – service and speedy delivery – technical counsel – these and many others can be foundations for a leadership position.

But what the manufacturer considers 'quality' is not one of them; it is only too often irrelevant, if not the manufacturer's alibi for turning out a marginal product that costs more but does not contribute anything different or better. There is no leadership if the market is not willing to recognize the claim. And that always means willingness to buy and to pay. Leadership position for a product or a business is an economic term rather than a moral or an aesthetic one.

Low price may be no criterion at all. (Indeed manufacturers' complaints that 'the trade' buys only by price and pays no attention to quality are often unfounded; the trade has definite value preferences and is willing to pay for them – the manufacturer just does not satisfy them.) But customer willingness to pay and customer purchases in preference to competitors' products are valid criteria of economic accomplishment in a competitive market economy. If they cannot be clearly demonstrated, a product must be suspected of being – or becoming – marginal.

In analysing products for their leadership position, the same questions should therefore always be asked: 'Is the product being bought in preference to other products on the market, or at least eagerly?' 'Do we have to give anything to get the customer to buy?' (e.g., the extraordinary amount of service which, as Table III [next page] shows, products F and G require). 'Do we get paid for what we deliver to him, as indicated by an at-least-average profit contribution?' 'Are we getting paid for what we think is the product distinction?' 'Or do we have a product with leadership position and with distinction without ourselves discerning it?' (as might well be the case with products C and D in the tables).

If the main products of a company show no signs of having such distinction and of occupying leadership position – as may be the case with Universal Products – it had better do something fast, especially if sales and profits seem to be doing well. Both sales and profits may suddenly collapse – yet no one is prepared, no one is forewarned, no one is working at restoring the leadership position of the products or developing new ones to replace what has become marginal.

Turning now to the prospects, Table II (page 37) summarized a lot of hard work – and even more internal disagreement. Judgements on prospects – on what can reasonably be expected of a product within the next few years – are, of course, fully as controversial as leadership position. One look at the table and every experienced executive knows that the prospect appraisal for product A will be bitterly disputed, especially by the engineering

TABLE III

UNIVERSAL PRODUCTS COMPANY PRODUCT ANALYSIS: PEOPLE

(dollars in millions)

| Product | Revenue | Quantity and Quality of Key Personnel Support | | |
		Managerial	*Technical*	*Sales and Service*
A	$19.0	Very high	Very good and plentiful	Very good and plentiful
B	14.0	Very high[a]	Very high[a]	Very high[a]
C	14.0	Good	Low	Medium in numbers and quality
D	11.0	High	Mediocre	Medium in numbers and quality
E	7.0	A nonentity	Many, but mediocre	Continuously high service demand
F	4.0 ⎫	Highly qualified technically	High in quality	Best salesmen— service high
G	4.0 ⎭			
H	3.5	Special task force	Our best people	High-pressure sales effort
I	2.0	Low	Low	Low in sales; high in service of old products in customer plants
J	Under 1.0	High	Quite high	Nil

[a] Two-thirds of the technically trained people appraised as 'superior or better' work on this product.

department, and that the dismal appraisal for product B is probably still too optimistic. He knows that the comptroller will challenge the high appraisal of the prospect for product D; whereas sales may want to push the estimate even higher. The expectation of continued sales for product I, even though on a very low level, is probably wishful thinking. The old-timers who made their careers designing, making and selling it still hope it will come back.

But what the analysis tries to do – and why it should be made – hardly needs explanation.

The amazing thing is that it is done so rarely. Individual products are frequently studied and their prospects assayed. Major markets too – e.g., the market for construction materials – may be studied, especially by the larger companies. But a searching look at the prospects of *all* the products at the same time, let alone of all result areas of a business, is still uncommon – even in companies that profess to believe in long-range planning. Yet it is both an easy thing to do – though not so easy to do well – and a most revealing, question-raising approach to the business and its capacity to perform and to produce results.

WHERE THE RESOURCES ARE

Actually I have got somewhat ahead of myself. In calling this or that product 'marginal', or in wondering whether another product might not have to give something 'extra' (e.g., heavy technical service) in order to retain its position, I have anticipated the results of the next step in the analysis: that of the allocation of key resources.

So far, by and large, the analysis has centred on things that happen to the business and its products. Now we ask what the business does to make things happen. Business has only two kinds of key resources: knowledge resources – that is, trained people – in buying, selling and servicing, in technical work, and especially in management; and money.

What are these scarce and expensive resources being used for? In what result areas are they deployed? Are they applied to opportunities or to problems? And to the important and most promising opportunities?

Tables III and IV show such an analysis of the resources allocation in Universal Products – though, of course, again in a fragmentary and grossly simplified form.

These resources have – or should have – the greatest impact. What really distinguishes a strong company from a weak one is above all its technical and professional people; its sales and service force; its managers, their knowledge, motivation and direction.

Knowledge-people, working capital, and operating expenses such as promotion money are also the only resources of a business that can be shifted from one job to another within reasonable time.

TABLE IV

UNIVERSAL PRODUCTS COMPANY PRODUCT ANALYSIS: MONEY

(dollars in millions)

Product	Revenue	Money Allocation as Percentage of Company Totals	
		Working Capital (Inventories and Receivables)	Promotion Expense
A	$19.0	15%) Together account for	25%
B	14.0	45%) 80% of receivables	40%
C	14.0	5%—Mostly inventories	Under 5%
D	11.0	3%—Mostly goods in transit	Nil
E	7.0	10%—Mostly repair parts	5%
F	4.0)	Almost nil—made to order	10%—Mostly
G	4.0)	and sold for cash	technical literature
H	3.5	15%—20% of all receivables	10%—Mostly special offers
I	2.0	5%—Mostly spares for obsolete models no longer made	5% to 7.5%— Trade-in allowance
J	Under 1.0	Nil	Yet to be budgeted

They are essentially the only 'manageable' resources. Capital investments, by contrast, are more or less immovable once the original investment decision has been made.

But precisely because these resources are so eminently manageable, they must be managed, or else they will inevitably be mismanaged. Their mobility makes them particularly susceptible to pressures and urgencies, as well as to drift.

No one is likely to say: 'Let's take our best plant, producing

our most profitable product, and loan it for six months to a
problem product; after all, the profitable product will still be
there six months hence.' But managements can say – indeed
do say all the time: 'Let's take our best design engineers working on a big new product for tomorrow, and loan them for six
months to spruce up an old, obsolescent model.' Or: 'Let's take
out some of the promotion money for the new product – it's
doing well anyhow; and we need a special campaign for the old
product that otherwise would be outdated fast by the new one.'

The danger of misallocation also applies to working capital
and to the 'managed' costs, especially promotion expense of all
kinds, from price discounts and technical literature to packaging
and advertising.

One consumer-goods company in the United States, producing and distributing a nationally branded line for household
use, found, for instance, that well over three-quarters of the
advertising budget went to the four products that were at best
near-failures. Four or five other products that contributed
the bulk of the company's revenue, had the best market, the
best growth potential and leadership, had to be satisfied
with an occasional mention. They should have occupied the
centre of the advertising effort.

Quantity is almost meaningless in respect to knowledge-people.
Their quality is far more important. What working capital or
promotion expenses are being used for is at least as important as
their amounts. Quantitative measurements such as budget figures
or manning tables therefore tell only a small part of the story. A
depth analysis is needed which shows both the quality of the resources allocated and their specific use or purpose.

The most effective industrial research director I know says:
'The number of competent research people grows only with the
square root of the total research group, the number of people
capable of sustained superior performance with the cube root
of the total.' To increase the number of superior research performers from three to ten, one therefore would have to increase
the size of the total group from thirty to a thousand. Most experienced men would concur in the general proposition that
the number of superior performers in any group – whether this
be skilled mechanics, doctors in a hospital, or professors at a
university – does not grow anywhere near as fast as the total

group. Any sales manager, any engineering manager, any comptroller, any faculty dean knows that one has to hire and train a great many 'boys' before one gets one 'man'.

It makes a great deal of difference what any one dollar of the manageable expenses is being spent on or invested in. A large inventory of spare parts needed because the product keeps breaking down and has to be fixed all the time may look the same on the books as a large inventory of finished products needed because demand is great. Similarly, it makes a difference in appraising performance of a piece of new equipment on the market, whether the promotion dollar goes to satisfy the demands of eager customers to have their personnel trained in using the product, or whether it goes to conceal substantial price cuts made to counteract customer-criticism and resistance.

An analysis of these resources and their allocation is therefore essential information for understanding the result areas.

The data on product E and its performance are made meaningful, for instance, by what the resources allocation analysis of Table III shows: the product is being 'managed' by the service men in the field rather than by a manager. And the performance of product H would have had to be interpreted quite differently had the resources allocation analysis shown it grossly lacking in key personnel support and money allocation.

This analysis is, in other words, also an essential step towards understanding, diagnosis and action-decision.*

There is a great deal more to knowledge and money resources than their allocation to result areas. But first one has to find out where these resources actually are and how they are related to business results.

---

* The analysis would, of course, be even more helpful if *total* capital employed could be related to result areas. This is possible, as a rule, only in the single-product company – or in a business which, like General Motors, has the bulk of its output in what is more or less one product in a small number of styles and sizes. However, total capital employed can usually be isolated whenever a larger business contains identifiable and separately managed smaller, decentralized businesses. There, of course, total capital allocation should be analysed, with return on total capital as the key to business appraisal (as in the DuPont formula).

4

How Are We Doing?

There are innumerable products and services on the market, each with its distinct properties and functions. There are hundreds of distinct markets and different end-uses, all kinds of ways to group customers, and many different channels to bring a product or service to its markets and customers.

Yet practically *all* products, markets and distributive channels can be classified under a small number of major categories. I have found eleven such categories adequate to classify all but the most exceptional cases.

The first five are fairly easy to diagnose. And the decision on their treatment is straightforward. They are:

1. Today's breadwinners;
2. Tomorrow's breadwinners;
3. Productive specialties;
4. Development products;
5. Failures.

The second group of six categories contains the problem children. They are:

6. Yesterday's breadwinners;
7. Repair jobs;
8. Unnecessary specialties;
9. Unjustified specialties;
10. Investments in managerial ego;
11. Cinderellas (or, sleepers).

How products might fit into these categories is shown in Table V which continues the schematic presentation of the Business X-ray of Universal Products.

There is, of course, no particular magic to the number eleven (and even less to the terms chosen). Some may prefer a few more categories or get by with fewer. (Repair jobs, unnecessary specialties, and unjustified specialties might all be combined, for instance.)

But every analysis, I believe, has found that all result areas can be classified in this way and that the classification largely decides what to do with a product, a market, or a distributive channel.

These few categories, in other words, give us a tentative diagnosis for all the result areas and for the business altogether.

1. *Today's breadwinners.* Products in this category always account for substantial volume. They also make an adequate, and

TABLE V

UNIVERSAL PRODUCTS COMPANY PRODUCT ANALYSIS:

A TENTATIVE DIAGNOSIS

(dollars in millions)

Product	Revenue	Diagnosis
A	$19.0	Today's breadwinner becoming *yesterday's breadwinner*. On way down. Considerably oversupported.
B	14.0	*Investment in managerial ego.* Withdraw *all* support?
C	14.0	*Today's breadwinner.* Inadequately supported to become 'tomorrow's breadwinner' and a leader.
D	11.0	Tomorrow's breadwinner. But will Prince Charming come before Cinderella gets old? Perhaps even a real 'sleeper'. NOT SUPPORTED.
E	7.0	*Repair job* needed on both product and management to cut out excessive service needs. Could then become a 'productive specialty', perhaps even a 'breadwinner'. Marginal today.
F G	4.0 ⎫ 4.0 ⎭	Necessary? Have neither product, leadership nor prospects. Are either nuclei of new main product or *'unjustified specialties'*.
H	3.5	Another *investment in managerial ego*.
I	2.0	The has-been. Breadwinner of the day before yesterday.
J	Under 1.0	Development. Not a product yet. Potential leader as new high-speed equipment comes into customers' plants. Do we know the market yet?

often a large, net revenue contribution. Their share of the cost burden should be at most no larger than their share in the revenues. Their contribution coefficient is good, though not commonly the highest. They still have some growth ahead, though usually only after considerable modification or change – in design, in pricing, in promotion, in selling methods, or in service. But even with modifications they are unlikely to grow much further. They are at their zenith or close to it.

Most company analyses turn up at least one product that is today's breadwinner. In this respect Universal Products is rather atypical in not having any one product that is clearly today's breadwinner. Product A is perilously close to becoming yesterday's breadwinner. And in its lack of adequate resources support, despite its growth potential, product C more nearly resembles tomorrow's breadwinner.

Today's breadwinner typically is amply supported by key resources. It actually should employ fewer key resources than its *present* revenue and profit contribution might seem to justify. It almost always employs more (in this respect product A is only too typical).

One reason for this common over-allocation of key resources to today's breadwinner is the belief that one can make it again into a growth product by putting a lot of effort behind it – even though everybody really knows that there is not much additional growth to be had. There is a tendency to consider a product today's breadwinner when, in reality, it has already become yesterday's breadwinner. Contribution coefficient is the best test (which product A would flunk).

2. *Tomorrow's breadwinners.* These are of course what everybody hopes all products are. And a company had better have at least one of them around. They are unfortunately not as common as company press releases and stock market letters assume. (Indeed, that Table V shows two candidates for this category – products C and D – among only ten products is rather higher than average.)

Tomorrow's breadwinner is both sizeable reality *and* promise. It already has a profitable, large market and wide acceptance. Yet its main growth is still ahead, without substantial changes in the product.

Net revenue contribution and contribution coefficient are typically high, are indeed typically higher than they should be. Because the product does so well, everybody thinks it does not need support. As a result, the key resources needed to make the most of it go elsewhere, especially to problems such as yesterday's breadwinner and above all to the investment in managerial ego. This is one of the worst ways of starving opportunities in order to feed the problems. For tomorrow's breadwinner is the product that gives the highest return on additional efforts and resources now.

Sometimes tomorrow's breadwinners are literally being starved to death. Or – all too often – there is just enough effort behind them to get them started but not enough to exploit them. The market is thus being readied for the competition to move in and reap the harvest without having done any sowing and cultivating. (This is likely to happen to product D in Table V, for instance, if it does not soon get the resources support it lacks.)

3. *Productive specialties* have both a limited and a distinct market. They should serve, however, a genuine function, should enjoy leadership in their market. Their net revenue contribution should be higher than their volume; their share in the cost burden, a good deal lower. And they should employ very limited resources, should indeed be almost by-products of the volume products.

Universal's product E might be made into a productive specialty – but it is not one yet.

4. *Development products.* Product J in Table V might serve as an example. It is not yet really a 'product'. It is still in process of introduction, if not in process of development. It has still to prove itself. But potential is considered great and hopes run high.

Development products deserve the best a company has, in terms of management, in terms of technical work, in terms of sales and service. But the number of people allocated to them should be small – though it will, of course, be larger than the revenue generated yet justifies.

The real problem of development products is not what they are and do today. It is to make sure that they do not turn into the worst of all product categories: investments in managerial ego.

5. *Failures.* These are not likely to be a problem of diagnosis or treatment. They announce themselves and they liquidate themselves.

Indeed, healthy businesses do not succumb even to serious failures, as shown by Ford's recovery from the Edsel car in 1957–58 (the most highly publicized product fiasco in American business history). Somehow failures are much like the pains small boys get from eating too many green apples. The pains are severe. There is danger, to be sure. But if a healthy boy survives the first thirty-six hours, he is almost certain to recover. By then the poison has liquidated itself.

THE PROBLEM CHILDREN

We now come to the second – and much more difficult – group.

6. *Yesterday's breadwinners*. Like today's breadwinners, products in this group tend to have large volume sales. But they no longer make a major contribution to profit. They are being kept in the market either by price cuts, by high pressure advertising and selling, or by special services, especially to small and scattered customers. In other words, their gross revenue tends to be low in relation to their volume, while the number of transactions needed to keep them alive is constantly growing.

Product A in Table V is, as said before, likely to qualify as one of yesterday's breadwinners. And the concentration of key resources on product A which the table shows is only too typical. Everyone in the business 'loves' yesterday's breadwinner; it is the 'product which built this company'. 'There's always going to be a demand for good old A' is an article of company faith. But yesterday's breadwinners are obsolescent. Soon they will be obsolete – and shortly thereafter as senile as product I in Table V. Nothing can prevent their decline. Even to slow it takes efforts which will not pay for themselves.

7. *Repair jobs*. To qualify for this category a product must satisfy a number of stringent requirements. It must have:
> Substantial volume.
> Considerable growth opportunities.
> A significant leadership position.
> High probability of exceptional results if successful.

But it suffers from *one – and only one –* major defect, which—
> Is clearly definable.
> Fairly easy to correct.
> Deprives the product of the full benefit of its profit and/or growth potential.

Product E in Table V looks like a repair job; if the service could be built into the product instead of being given as an 'extra' and as an incentive to buy, the product could become a respectable and profitable productive specialty. With some volume growth, it might even turn into a breadwinner, that is, into a profitable volume line. What it lacks is clear enough; it has no management.

Repair jobs tend to be sold to the wrong customers – or not offered to the right ones – or moved through the wrong distributive channel. More would therefore turn up if we were to analyse these other result areas.

In Universal Products, for example, a repair job identified in the market analysis revived the has-been product I. The very feature that made it obsolete in the United States market made it almost ideal for the company's Latin American businesses. They needed a product simple in application and suitable for small plants and fairly slow equipment. The company's three manufacturing subsidiaries in Latin America were rapidly losing profitability despite market leadership; they had no cheap product with which to meet the competition of a European product designed for small plants employing a few highly skilled technicians and simple machinery.

The repair job here took the form of discontinuing domestic manufacture of product I and starting to make it in all three Latin American subsidiaries. The few United States customers who still want it have it shipped from the Mexican subsidiary; but no one tries to sell it in the United States market. In Latin America, however, this product has become today's bread-winner for all three subsidiaries, with the Mexican company exporting it all over the Caribbean, in addition. These export sales alone, a few years after the start of production in Mexico, were larger than the parent company sales of the product when it was made only in the United States.

Here is an example of a distributive channel repair job:

Having just started door-to-door selling, a producer of home-maintenance equipment was pleased with the results. Compared to other companies his salesmen had an exception-ally favourable ratio of buying customers to number of calls and sold three times as much per sale. Further analysis brought out, however, that the operation produced a substantial loss. While the salesmen sold more per call than other door-to-door salesmen, they made only a fraction of the calls. Instead of completing a call in a few minutes they would have to stay hours, demonstrating their products, counselling on specific home-repair or -maintenance problems, and so on. And when, upon orders from the head office, they cut their calls short, sales disappeared.

The repair necessary was to give the salesmen more products to sell so as to get a much larger sale per call. The company actually made such products, including some with a fairly high unit price. But it had intentionally withheld them from door-to-door selling in the belief that only low-cost items (and few of them at a time) could be sold at the door. When it gave the door-to-door salesmen the full line (and a small truck to carry it on) sales per call went up several times in a few months.

Beware however! Not everything in trouble is a repair job – indeed, few products are. The requirements spelled out for it must be rigidly enforced. If a product fails to meet a single one, it should be rejected out of hand as a repair job. Otherwise, every yesterday's breadwinner, every unjustified specialty, above all every investment in managerial ego will claim to belong.

And under no circumstances should there be more than one repair operation on a repair job. If the repair does not work the first time, the plea 'now we know what's *really* wrong here' should be most unsympathetically received. A repair job is bad enough; but an investment in managerial ego is worse. Yet this is what a 'second chance' for the repair job will produce in the majority of cases.

8. *Unnecessary specialties*. But for its clumsiness, a better name would be 'The specialty that needn't be one'. For what is unnecessary here is the existence of specialties instead of one successful main product with enough volume to yield results.

> Over the years an enormous number of special designs had been developed for fractional horsepower motors – each of them, it seemed at the time, serving a specific and slightly different need. As a result there was, in this industry, endless diversity. In reality the traditional classification of small motors had become obsolescent. But no new standardization had been attempted. When it was finally put through, during the last ten years, the apparently endless variety in the field reduced itself to five, six, or seven categories, each of them a major volume product.

One common symptom of unnecessary specialties is that half a dozen different ones are available for every customer or market requirement. Wherever a customer's need might be satisfied just as well with any of a half-dozen variations – all specialties – a new 'ordinary' volume product is likely to be hidden. Another sign is that advances in technology can be applied across the whole range of products, though each pretends to be a specialty for one 'special' purpose.

Products F and G in Table V may be unnecessary specialties. Judged by revenue contribution they certainly are not productive specialties.

To have unsatisfactory results is not enough to make a product qualify as an unnecessary specialty, however. There must also be a real opportunity – for sales, for profits, for growth – for the future, new main product that is to supersede the clutter of specialties.

Otherwise we just have another unjustified specialty.

9. *Unjustified specialties.* An unjustified specialty is one which does not really fulfil an economic function in the market place. It is meaningless differentiation for which the customer is not willing to pay.

The product on which a major maker of laboratory equipment prided himself was such an unjustified specialty: a microscope which was only a little different from standard instruments but cost much more because it required different production and different finishing. But it was not sufficiently different to obtain a premium price. Instead it generated almost three-quarters of all complaints and required heavy service support. It was just sufficiently different to need special handling and people trained in its temper tantrums. Yet because it was expensive and difficult to make it was considered a quality product. Only the customers did not share the illusion.

It is indeed easy to discover the unjustified specialty. Since the customer does not pay for it, its profit performance is poor. And since he usually does not want it either, complaints and service calls run high. But the unjustified specialty will always be defended with the argument, 'If we didn't have it, we wouldn't get the order for the volume products.' Sometimes the plea is valid – but in that case the specialty is not a 'product' but the promotional part of a 'package'. More often, however, there is little substance to the defence. Sales-people frequently push a customer who wants a standard product into ordering a 'special' with the argument: 'Look at all the extra features you get free.'

Specialties in the case of a producer of metal products in Great Britain accounted for 20 per cent of volume but for something like 70 per cent of cost. They were stoutly defended by the entire sales department as necessary to attract and hold the customers for the main products. When, however, a supply of the main products from the continent of Europe became available at a slightly lower price, the main-product customers immediately switched over to the new and slightly cheaper source of supply. The British company was left with its specialties. The irony was that the British company, despite the higher prices on its main products, was losing money because of the transactional costs of the specialties; whereas the continental supplier, despite lower prices and high capital costs, was making money fast.

Whether the buyers of main products actually buy the specialty is the best test, in other words – though it should be made before they stop buying the main grades. It is common for a specialty to have its own small, scattered customers while the volume customers shun it.

Unjustified specialties are always a drain on a company's results. They absorb a disproportionate amount of key resources. They require, as a rule, constant technical work to modify and diversify even further. For they can be kept in the market only if made to look 'new' and different. Not being standard products, production runs are short and expensive, quality is not too predictable, and performance not closely controllable. As a result unjustified specialties typically produce a crop of complaints and constant service calls.

Much more dangerous, much more common, and infinitely harder to get rid of is the next category:

10. *Investments in managerial ego* (of which products B and H in Table V are examples).

This is the product that should be a success – but is not. But management has invested so much in the product by way of pride and skill that it refuses to face reality. The product, management is convinced, will succeed tomorrow – but tomorrow never comes. And the longer the product fails to live up to expectations, the more does management become addicted to it, and the more key resources are pumped into it.

I mentioned earlier Ford's Edsel venture as the most publicized American product fiasco. Actually the Edsel was the kind of failure that cannot, as a rule, be foreseen and prevented. What made it a big failure was simply that Ford is a very big company and the automobile market a very big market. And

Ford dropped the Edsel fast and recovered rapidly without lasting ill-effects.

But few people outside the automobile industry realize that another automobile company was nearly destroyed by clinging for almost a quarter-century to an investment in managerial ego. This car was launched with hopes as great as those that led to the launching of the Edsel. It did not, however, fail as completely. It was a near-failure rather than a total one. For a quarter-century every survey showed that the car was the best engineered car, that it was styled and priced for the largest share of the market, and that the American public loved it.

The only thing wrong was that the American public did not buy it. Year after year this car failed in the market. But the forecasts for next year were always that it would finally take off and become the successful leader to which its qualities 'entitled' it. To this end the company not only poured in more and more money. Worse, its key resources – managerial, technical and marketing – were all sacrificed to this near-failure. As soon as anybody in the company showed any ability, he was plucked out of whatever job he was doing – especially, if he worked on pushing the successful cars made by the company – and allocated to this 'sick child'. And six months or a year later, after he too had failed to make the car into a success, he usually became a former employee of the company.

When, after twenty-five years, the car was finally dropped, it had all but sucked dry what had been a powerful, successful and growing company.

This example brings out the attitudes that create investments in managerial ego: the attitude that a product is 'entitled' to success (or to its 'proper price'); and the certainty that a product, and especially a new one, 'must' succeed because 'we know it is the best quality'.

Both beliefs are, of course, poor economics. Moreover, they violate the most elementary probabilities. The odds against any new product's becoming even a moderate success are roughly five to one, and the odds against its becoming a smash hit are one hundred to one.

We know that out of every one hundred new products or services one, on average, becomes a real success and the foundation of a substantial and profitable business. Another nineteen or so become respectable breadwinners or productive specialties without ever becoming spectacular.

We also know that one of every hundred new products and services is as spectacular a failure as was the Edsel. One, in other words, liquidates itself immediately. Nineteen others fade before they have done serious damage.

This leaves sixty of the new products and services that, in all probability, will neither become successes to the point where they really earn their keep, nor turn into failures blatant enough to be abandoned. Sixty out of every hundred new products and services have therefore to be pruned lest they become investments in managerial ego.

The greatest self-delusion is the belief that the outlook for a product improves the more resources are poured into it.

Few popular maxims are as wide of the mark as, 'If at first you don't succeed, try, try, try again.' 'If at first you don't succeed, try once more – and then try something else' is more realistic. Success in repetitive attempts becomes less rather than more probable with each repetition.

Every new product has to be given a limited time to come up to expectations. It should get an extension only if it has made great progress. If it still does not come through after such an extension. it should not be given another chance. Otherwise the business will become overgrown with investments in managerial ego, absorbing key resources, taking an exorbitant amount of management time – and yet never doing better.

The only industry that seems to understand this is book publishing. If a new novel has not succeeded within a short time, publishers stop advertising and promoting it. And another six months later they sell out the remaining stock and take their loss. Contrary to popular legend no masterpiece ever suffered oblivion because of this practice.

Managerial ego is also normally involved in the next and last category:

11. *Cinderellas* – or, less poetically, *sleepers*. These products might do well if only they were given a chance. Instead they do not get the supply and key resources their performance has already earned.

Product D in Table V looks like such a sleeper. The comment

on its leadership position also brings out why its opportunity is not being exploited.

One reason is the common management mistake of identifying profit margin with profit which is always profit margin multiplied by turnover. And profit margin needs adjustment to the transactions a product generates – as against the averaging of the cost burden common in accounting figures. Profit margins can also be deceptive where raw materials contents differ between products. A profit margin of $1.00 on $10-product A yields five times the profit of the $2.00 margin on $10-product B, if A sells ten times as much as B in the same time. Every businessman knows this, of course – but he remembers it only when (as in the DuPont and General Motors formulae for return on investment) turnover and margin are always associated and appear together (or are, as in the revenue figures used in our analysis, expressed together in one result figure).

The second reason why product D is disliked may be more important. It gets the sales that product B 'was designed for'. Its success threatens management's favourite. Other Cinderellas may encroach on today's breadwinner or speed the decline of yesterday's breadwinner. And since managers are human beings, they hope that this uncomfortable threat will go away if only one pays no attention to it. What is likely to happen instead is that a competitor – often a complete outsider to the industry – discovers Cinderella and elopes with her, leaving behind both today's breadwinner and its producer.

The developers of the transistor in the early fifties were American companies which had a large and profitable business in electronic tubes, especially in supplying replacement tubes for radio and television sets. The new transistor did the job of the electronic tube at a fraction of the cost, weighed little, and required neither energy nor space. While it was thus a definite threat to the tube, it generated no replacement business. It is only too understandable that, in this situation, the people in the large American companies felt that the transistor was 'not yet ready' for general use. The Japanese, however, had no stake in the *status quo*. They realized that the low cost, light weight, small energy and space requirements of the transistor made possible a truly portable small radio. They took the American transistor, the same transistor that was not yet ready, and built on it their big radio business in the American market.

Not every new product that goes without support is a sleeper. But if a product does much better than expected despite lack of support, it may be one. There is a prima-facie case for increasing its key resources support, and especially for upgrading the quality of the key resources allocated to the product. At least the product has shown a greater potential than anybody had predicted.

DIAGNOSING THE CHANGING PRODUCT

To classify products as well as the other result areas is not too difficult. But it is not enough for a valid diagnosis.

We also need to be able to anticipate a change in the character of a product, especially a degenerative one. How can we tell when tomorrow's breadwinner turns into today's breadwinner and goes on to become yesterday's breadwinner? How can we tell that yesterday's development product is on the way to becoming an investment in managerial ego, and so on?

Two simple rules apply to all classifications in all result areas (except the outright failures which take care of themselves):

1. Any significant deviation of performance from expectations is likely to signal a change in classification. At least it demands re-analysis.

2. There is a 'life cycle' to every product (market, end-use, distributive channel). Analysis of the *cost of further increments of growth* shows where a product stands in its life cycle and what its life expectancy is.

The first rule requires that expectations be written down ahead of events.

The human memory is singularly elastic. Three years later nobody remembers that a product was once expected to revolutionize the industry, instead of which it just barely returns its operating expenses. What everybody is likely to remember is, 'We started this as a minor addition to our product line and it is doing quite well.' Only insistence on writing out expectations for a product can therefore provide a reliable record.

By comparing the actual course of events against expectations, we can identify in particular two major problem areas: the degenerative disease of the investment in managerial ego and the missed opportunity of the sleeper. Holding performance against expectations is also the best way to find the unjustified speciality. For, almost without exception, it comes into being in the expectation that it will produce exceptionally high profits, or grow into a major product, or create a new major market, or at least that it will bring in new major customers for the volume products.

INCREMENTAL ANALYSIS

The idea of a life cycle for a product making possible incremental analysis is, unlike that of an expectations-result comparison, a new one to most businessmen. It therefore deserves some explanation.

The life-span of products is so different as to make any generalization impossible. Some products last only a few months or years. Aspirin, on the other hand, in an industry noted for its rapid change and high rate of innovation, has lasted, little changed, for seventy years now and shows few signs of getting old and tired.

Yet no product lasts for ever. And the pattern of its life cycle is always the same. In its infancy, a product requires high inputs of resources without any return. This is actually the stage before it becomes a 'product'. It is only a 'development'.

When it reaches its youth, each additional dollar of new input should produce many dollars in return – whether the additional input is in the form of capital, of technical improvement, or of key resources. When the product reaches maturity and becomes today's breadwinner, the incremental acquisition to be gained by additional input goes down sharply; where the cost of incremental acquisition reaches or exceeds the additional revenue that can be acquired, a product becomes yesterday's breadwinner. The investment in managerial ego, however, goes straight from early youth into senile decline where additional efforts cost more than they return.

There exists for this a simple mathematical theorem familiar to any engineer. At one point – the engineer calls it the 'knee of the curve' – the increments of output begin to decrease rapidly. Up to that point, for instance, the increment of output to be obtained by each additional unit of input has been going down in arithmetic progression, from ten, to nine, to eight, to seven, and so on. Suddenly these increments begin to go down in geometric progression. For each additional unit of input, for instance, one only gets one-half or less as much additional output as the preceding increment produced. At this point inputs are actually no longer productive. Returns are diminishing too fast. At this point one, therefore, stops further inputs.*

One should actually stop further inputs before the output gain for each incremental input unit starts to go down. This, in terms of the life cycle, is the point where a product becomes today's breadwinner. It is the optimum point. It corresponds to the optimum driving speed in an automobile or the optimum flying speed of an airplane – where one gets the most performance from the fuel, the most results from the resources.

The concept of the cost of incremental acquisition does not apply only to individual products or service, markets or customers. A sharp rise in the cost of incremental acquisitions is usually the first, but also the most significant, danger signal for an entire business or industry.

That the mass-circulation magazines in the United States were headed for trouble was signalled, for instance, in the early 'fifties, by a sharp rise in the cost of incremental acquisition of new subscriptions. To raise their circulation further, magazines had suddenly to spend more than they got back in additional subscription fees. At that time the mass-circulation magazines seemed headed for larger revenues and better business. Yet the crisis that within a few years wiped out a good many of them, and still threatens to kill more, could already be foreseen. Not being able to reverse the trend in the cost of incremental additions to circulation, the mass-magazines had to run into trouble.

Advertising, sales and promotion expenses are particularly suited to this analysis. How much additional business does each additional million dollars of advertising generate? Actually, advertising in which the incremental yields do not go up as advertising expenditure incrۮases is, in all probability, uneconomic advertising. It is not enough for the increments to remain steady. They must still go up. This is simply another way of saying what

* One application of this theorem with which many executives *are* familiar is statistical sampling. A sample is optimal when enlarging it no longer increases the reliability of the findings by a statistically significant amount.

any advertising man knows: Advertising is either superbly effective – or it is no good at all.

Applied to the present situation in the United States, this would raise serious doubts regarding the most popular advertising medium, television. There, for the last ten years, it has only been possible to increase the money spent. But in so far as figures are available, it does not seem that any additional results have been obtainable.

The importance and applicability of the concept of the cost of incremental acquisitions go way beyond the scope of this chapter. This concept applies to a great many business tasks over and beyond that of making the present business effective. Indeed, it is one of the most important diagnostic tools at our disposal. That modern accounting is rapidly recognizing this fact and is organizing its system to provide the needed figures for incremental analysis is a major improvement in management's performance capacity. Incremental analysis converts the tentative diagnosis from an audit of the past into a tool of anticipation and prevention.

5

Cost Centres and Cost Structure

Costs – their identification, measurement and control – are the most thoroughly worked, if not overworked, business area. In this vineyard labour the most, the busiest, and the best equipped of the business professions: accountants, industrial engineers, methods analysts, operations researchers, and so on. The Anglo-American economist in his 'theory of the firm' is primarily interested in costs, their character and their control. And so is the German with his *Betriebswirtschaftslehre*. An enormous amount of work goes into cost control, an enormous amount of time goes to cost analysis. There is no lack of tools, of techniques, of books on the subject.

The annual cost-reduction drive, for instance, is as predictable in most businesses as a head cold in spring. It is about as enjoyable. But six months later costs are back where they were – and the business braces itself for the next cost-reduction drive.

The one important exception is the cost-reduction 'miracle' of a new management in a sadly run-down company. The company typically has enjoyed leadership, if not monopoly position under an earlier, hard-driving management. Under weak successors it has drifted unmanaged until it found itself suddenly face to face with total ruin. Then costs can be slashed by one-third or by one-half by doing the obvious – by closing down, for instance, an old plant that for years has turned out neither products nor profits. But this also means that the cost-reduction miracle at best provides a breathing spell during which the new management can begin rebuilding the business.

Altogether focusing resources on results is the best and most effective cost control. Cost, after all, does not exist by itself. It is always incurred – in intent at least – for the sake of a result. What matters therefore is not the absolute cost level but the ratio between efforts and their results. No matter how cheap or efficient an effort, it is waste, rather than cost, if it is devoid of results. And if it was incapable of producing results all along, it was unjustifiable waste from the beginning. Maximizing opportunities is therefore the principal road to a high effort/result ratio and with it to cost control and low costs. It must come first; other cost-control efforts are additional rather than central.

Yet even a business that works systematically on directing its efforts and resources towards opportunities and results needs cost analysis and cost control. No business can possibly run without frittering away efforts – just as no machine on earth can be made to run without friction losses. But a business and its cost performance can be greatly improved, just as friction can be reduced.

There are several prerequisites for effective cost control:

1. Concentration must centre on controlling the costs where they are. It takes approximately as much effort to cut 10 per cent off a cost item of $50,000 as it does to cut 10 per cent off a cost item of $5 million. Costs, too, in other words are a social phenomenon, with 90 per cent or so of the costs incurred by 10 per cent or so of the activities.

2. Different costs must be treated differently. Costs vary enormously in their character – as do products.

3. The one truly effective way to cut costs is to cut out an activity altogether. To try to cut back costs is rarely effective. There is little point in trying to do cheaply what should not be done at all.

Typically, however, the cost-cutting drive starts with a declaration by management that no activity or department is to be abolished. This condemns the whole exercise to futility. It can only result in harming essential activities – and in making sure that the unessential ones will be back at full, original cost level within a few months.

4. Effective control of costs requires that the whole business be looked at – just as all the result areas of a business have to be looked at to gain understanding.

Otherwise, costs will be reduced in one place by simply being pushed somewhere else. This looks like a great victory for cost reduction – until the final results are in a few months later, with total costs as high as ever.

There is, for example, the cost reduction in manufacturing which is achieved by pushing the burden of adjustment on the shipping-room and the warehouse. There is cost reduction of inventory which pushes costs of uncontrolled fluctuation upstream onto manufacturing. There is, typically, a great cost reduction in the price of some purchased material which, however, results in longer, slower and costlier machine work to handle the less than perfect substitute material. These examples, as every manager knows, could be continued almost *ad infinitum*.

5. 'Cost' is a term of economics. The cost system that needs to be analysed is therefore the entire *economic* activity which produces economic value.

'Cost' should be defined as what the customer pays to obtain certain goods or services and to derive full utility from them. It is, however, almost always defined legally rather than economically; that is, as those expenses which occur within a particular – and purely arbitrary – legal entity, the individual business. This leaves out the bulk of the true costs. Two-thirds of the cost of every single product or service lies outside any one particular business. The manufacturer accounts for at most one-quarter of the customer's cost – the rest goes for the raw material the manufacturer purchases, for the expenses of a converter or fabricator, and, of course, for the costs of distribution which normally accrue in the legally independent and different businesses of wholesaler and retailer. The retailer – the department store, for instance – is again responsible only for a small part of the total costs – the main costs are those of the goods he buys in order to sell them, and so on. What matters, however, to the customer, and what determines whether he buys or not, is total outlay. He is completely unconcerned with how the outlay is divided between a number of legally independent businesses in the economic chain from raw material to finished article. All he is concerned with is what he pays for what he gets.

'Cost control' that limits itself to the costs incurred within any of the legal entities in the economic chain can never hope to control costs. At the least, cost control demands that the entire costs be known and understood.

Indeed the definition of 'costs' might go beyond customer purchases. No one buys a thing. He buys the satisfaction and utility he derives therefrom. True economic costs therefore should include everything the customer has to spend to derive the full use from his purchase – in maintenance, in repair, in running costs, and so on.

It does not follow that an article can be sold for more money if only its maintenance costs are sufficiently lowered. It may well be that the customer's own situation forces him to define 'price' as initial outlay and to disregard cost of upkeep. In the United States and in England, for instance, municipalities as a rule have stringent restrictions on their borrowing powers but fairly broad taxing powers. They can therefore afford to pay higher operating costs which are defrayed out of taxes provided only that capital costs, normally provided out of borrowings, are kept low. As a result, municipalities in these two countries have been reluctant to buy aluminium poles for street lighting, which over their twenty-year life are cheaper than steel poles but cost more in terms of initial purchase. And no matter what the economic realities, they will be disregarded as long as the legal rules under which these customers operate impose on them what may be economically speaking irrational behaviour.

A cost analysis therefore is not truly meaningful or reliable unless reviewed and revised against the findings of a *marketing* analysis that looks at the business from the outside. By itself it is only a partial view.

In some of the most conspicuously successful businesses the work done on outside costs is the real key to their accomplishment.

The two retail giants who are the 'distribution successes' of America and England respectively – Sears Roebuck in the United States and Marks & Spencer in England – are examples. Both owe their success above all to finding manufacturers, developing new and improved manufacturing processes for their suppliers, and specifying the costs of the manufacturers' finished products. Both have taken active responsibility for the manufacturer's costs, products and processes well beyond, and outside, their legal control.

Similarly, the success of General Motors rests to a large extent on the company's work on the cost structure of the independent automobile dealer. IBM owes much of its success to engineering of the customer's paperwork so as to make the equipment most productive.

To be able to control costs, a business therefore needs a *cost analysis* which:

Identifies the *cost centres* – that is, the areas where the significant costs are, and where effective cost reduction can really produce results.

Finds what the important *cost points* are in each major cost centre.

Looks at the entire business as one *cost stream*.

Defines 'cost' as what the customer pays rather than as what the legal or tax unit of accounting incurs.

Classifies costs according to their basic characteristics and thus produces a *cost diagnosis*.

TYPICAL COST CENTRES

Where are the cost centres in the business and its economic process? Where is it really worth while to work on the control of costs? Where, in other words, could a relatively minor improvement in cost have really significant results for the total costs of the business? And which are the areas where even substantial improvement would really not mean much in terms of the total costs of economic performance?

An analysis by cost centres for Universal Products is shown in Table VI. These figures are crude, to be sure, and they are not intended to be representative of every type of business. They are only intended to indicate where to look further.

Money (in the manufacturer's business as well as in those of the distributors) and *physical movement of materials and goods* account together for 36 per cent of the total or for more than half of all costs after raw materials. This is quite typical. Yet these two areas tend to be overlooked as cost centres.

Cost of money in the business, a financial analyst might argue, is actually a good deal higher than shown. It probably includes most of what is shown as profits which are actually costs of capital needed to stay in business. There is merit to this position – accepting it would make the cost of money the largest of all cost centres.

Money in the business is always a major cost centre. It is also the one cost area where efforts are easiest and are most likely to produce meaningful results. It is, as a rule, easier to speed up the turnover of money than to do much about unsatisfactory profit margins. Yet only in the last few years have American managements taken seriously the management of money in the business. Indeed, this job has only recently been accepted as an important function of management, for which somebody in the top group has to be responsible, and on which somebody has to work full time. Moreover, businesses specifically fail to think through the financial structure that is most appropriate for their economics,

TABLE VI

UNIVERSAL PRODUCTS COMPANY: TOTAL COSTS AND COST STRUCTURE[a]

THE CONSUMER'S DOLLAR		100%
I. *Physical movement of materials and goods*		
(a) From materials supplier to factory; from warehouse to machines and through factory	6%	
(b) From machines as finished goods through packaging, crating, shipping, warehousing to wholesaler	6%	17%
(c) By distributors (wholesale and retail)	5%	
II. *Selling and sales promotion* (manufacturer, wholesaler, and retailer)		8%
III. *Cost of money in the manufacturer's business – including working capital, interest charges, depreciation, and mainte-nance of equipment* (manufacturer only)		13%
IV. *Cost of money for distributors* (rough estimate)		6%
V. *Manufacturing – conversion of materials into saleable products*		9%
VI. *Purchased materials and supplies*		25%
VII. *Management, administration and record keeping* (manufacturer, wholesaler and retailer)		10%
VIII. *Investment in tomorrow* – research, market development, executive development, and so on		2%
IX. PROFITS – before taxes – of manufacturer, wholesaler and retailer (but excluding, as unknown, profits of materials suppliers)		10%

[a] The actual analysis—here reproduced in simplified form—showed, of course, ranges rather than absolute figures; i.e., the figure for Physical Movement was 13-19 per cent rather than 17 per cent.

and that gives them the best utilization of that most expensive 'raw material', money. Typically, at least in the United States, businesses use equity money to finance bankable loans, though it is elementary that one cannot make an equity return on a bankable loan.

Until a few years ago, one of the major food processing companies in the United States, canning such seasonal products as tomatoes, peas, or corn, financed itself entirely through equity capital. But vegetables have to be canned when they ripen and have then to be kept on the shelves the rest of the year. Equity capital, in other words, was put into commodities and left idle for many months – where bank loans at the lowest prevailing rates of interest would have been easily obtainable. As a result this company became less profitable the more it grew – to the point where it almost succeeded in killing itself through too much success.

Similarly, it is common to find businesses using permanent indebtedness for purely seasonal demands – for instance, long-term notes for fluctuating inventories. They thus pay interest all year for money they use two to three months. It is common to find companies that are 'real estate poor', having sunk tremendous amounts of equity capital into real estate of, at best, marginal productivity, real estate they should either not have at all or should finance through conventional mortgage or insurance-company money.

Altogether it can be said that any dogmatic financial policy is likely to be wrong. It is as wrong to say, 'We do not believe in debt', as to say, 'We borrow every penny we can get.' The right way to manage money is to think through the economics of the business and to finance accordingly. Few things are as expensive as the wrong financial structure. Few things, however, are so completely hidden in the traditional approach to costs – and so totally beyond the reach of the conventional cost reduction drive.

But the costs of money in the business are also often inflated by economically misleading conventions, especially those of the tax regulations. The tax distinction between capital investments and operating expenses creates, for instance, hidden costs. It is a legal rather than an economic distinction. Economically, capital investment may be considered as the present value of future income expectations; while maintenance and depreciation are nothing but the instalments through which capital investment is paid for. The cost centre is therefore always total cost of capital, regardless of whether this is shown as operating expense, e.g., maintenance, in the profit and loss statement, or as capital investment in the balance sheet, regardless, in other words, of whether this is shown as a cost or as an asset. Which costs the least amount of money (tax included) is the only appropriate criterion.

None of this can be deduced from looking at the figures of Table VI.

The one suspicion they raise immediately, however, is that the company finances its distributors heavily – though whether this is actually the case and whether it serves a purpose, cannot yet be said.

Distribution is always a major cost centre – and is generally neglected. One reason is that distribution costs are spread among all the businesses in the entire economic process. And much distributive cost is incurred between two businesses in the process and is left untended by both. Another reason is that distribution costs within a business tend to be hidden in a great many places rather than shown together as the cost of a major economic activity. Moving goods and storing them are parts of the same distributive activity. Their costs may be shown in 'miscellaneous' under many headings.

Inside the manufacturing plant there are, for instance, the costs incurred between finished production, i.e., the stage at which a product comes off the machine, and its shipment to a customer. These costs include cutting, labelling, packaging, storing, moving. This is usually considered 'manufacturing overhead'; nobody is really accountable for the activity. But inventories outside of the plant are usually considered 'working capital' and their costs a 'cost of money'.

The costs of physical distribution are likely to yield to cost-reduction and cost-control efforts much more readily than manufacturing costs, simply because so much less effort has been directed at them.

Warehousing, for instance, is a sizeable cost point in many businesses (as well as in such distribution systems as those of the Armed Forces). In some industries it runs to 8 per cent or more of total cost to the consumer. In all but the most modern mechanized warehouse, labour accounts for the main warehousing costs. Yet in many warehouses, owned and run by companies that pride themselves on their industrial engineering in the plant, labour costs are almost twice what they need to be. They still use the traditional gang system where three or four people work together on a task that actually only one man can do; for instance, unloading a railroad car or truck. There is only room for one man in the car; all the other members of the gang stand around and wait. Forty to 60 per cent of workers' time under the gang system is normally wasted, standing and waiting.

In the plant such waste would long ago have been seen and corrected.

Raw Materials in a manufacturing business are also almost always a cost centre of first magnitude. They need to be treated the way an effective large retailer finds, selects and buys the goods it resells. It is not enough to buy a certain material cheaply and in good quality. The cost-impact of raw materials is such that their selection should be part of product design. The manufacturer, in respect to a material or a part, is the distributive channel. The material must fit his product, but the product must also be designed to fit the available materials. Both must be integrated so that the best product performance is obtained from that material which, in the total process of fabrication and distribution, costs the least.

This is what people have in mind when they speak of 'materials management' instead of 'purchasing'. There are a good many techniques for the job available now; for instance, Value Engineering, which looks at each part of a product and asks of it: 'What is the simplest and least expensive way to do this particular job?' Some of the large buyers – for instance, the automobile companies – have become highly sophisticated materials managers and fully integrate design and purchasing. But most manufacturers still have to learn what some of the large retailers grasped thirty or forty years ago: Buying is as important as selling; and the best selling cannot make up for a mediocre buying specification.

By contrast, the cost of manufacturing – that is, the cost of doing something physically to change the composition, shape, configuration, or appearance of physical substances – is not a major cost centre.

Manufacturing is the one area where systematic and continuing work on cost control, that of the industrial engineer, has been going on for a long time. In most industries genuine manufacturing costs have become such a small part of total costs that significant cost-cutting requires a genuine breakthrough in manufacturing technology.

Such a breakthrough might emerge from a major change in the entire manufacturing process, such as automation; that is, a much higher degree of mechanization in doing the work itself, in handling and moving material and work, and in information and control of process.

But it might also lie in going in the opposite direction towards less integration of process and greater flexibility. In a good many process industries – for instance, aluminium rolling or paper-making – real breakthroughs have been achieved by uncoupling the manufacturing from the finishing process. An aluminium rolling mill, for example, physically separated the rolling of aluminium from its cutting, colouring and shaping. Similarly, in a large paper mill, a significant breakthrough was achieved by separating the production of paper base-stock from the finishing process, coating, cutting, and so on. In both cases inventories that used to be in the form of finished goods are now kept as semi-finished material between manufacturing and finishing, with great reductions in total inventory needs and yet with significant improvement in the ability to satisfy grade and delivery requirements of customers.

Sometimes the most significant breakthrough is to shut down a plant even though it is 'as good as new'. The plant may be the wrong size or it may be in the wrong location – or it may, altogether, be no longer appropriate.

The most important cost contribution in manufacturing may lie in organizing the process according to its economic character rather than according to tradition. A paper mill, typically, tends to be organized so as to utilize pulp optimally. But pulp is only one of the basic materials of papermaking. Temperature is expensive too. And so are the chemicals that make the paper white or opaque to light, that give it the required printing surface it needs, and so on. To organize the papermaking process around the utilization of heat and chemicals rather than as a process for converting pulp at the lowest cost and greatest speed may significantly change the economics of paper manufacturing. And the same rethinking of the materials-balance around which manufacturing is organized can be applied to other industries and processes.

Short of such a breakthrough, not much is to be gained from cost reduction in manufacturing – in any one company or in well-managed plants altogether. Yet this is where the trained force of industrial engineers is usually concentrated. And a good many managements believe that they control costs by watching day-to-day fluctuations in manufacturing cost-ratios.

THE COST POINTS

Cost points are simply the few activities within a cost centre that are responsible for the bulk of its costs. Again the assumption is that a few activities will account for the bulk of the costs. Major cost points are of course those activities which account for the transactions on which cost-calculations in any result area analysis are based. (See Chapters 2 and 3.)

Table VII shows such an analysis for major cost centres.

Some of these results were expected by management. Among them were:

Item	*Per Cent of Customer Dollar*
4 Packaging and crating	3
7 Finished goods inventories of manufacturer	3
11 Material A	5
12 Material B	5

But most results came as a distinct surprise. Particularly upsetting – being much larger than anybody had realized – were:

Item	*Per Cent of Customer Dollar*
3 Handling in warehouses	4
8 Receivables	$2\frac{1}{2}$
10 Inventories in dealer's hands	$1\frac{1}{2}$
13 Packaging materials	5
14 Order handling	3
15 Credit and collections	2

Promotion – item 6 – on the other hand, had been thought to run much higher; the company's dealers actually left promotion to the manufacturer when they had been expected to match his efforts. And while the size of the receivables had of course been known, their relationship to inventories confirmed the suspicion that the company was indeed not only financing the distribution of its own products but was financing the distributor himself

TABLE VII

UNIVERSAL PRODUCTS COMPANY: COST POINTS

Major Cost Centre	Cost Points	Percentage of Cost Centre Costs	Percentage of Customer Dollar
I. PHYSICAL MOVEMENT of materials and goods	1. TRANSPORTATION INSIDE and between plants	15%	2.5%
	2. TRANSPORTATION to and from OUTSIDE and plants	26	4
	3. HANDLING in SHIPPING ROOMS and WAREHOUSES	24	4
	4. Packaging and crating	20	3
II. SELLING (manufacturer, wholesaler, retailer)	5. Salesmen	62	5
	6. Promotion	25	2
III. COST OF MONEY	7. INVENTORIES of finished goods, especially in warehouses	23	3
	8. Receivables	20	2.5
	9. Interest	9	1
IV. COST OF MONEY (distributors)	10. Inventories	25	1.5
VI. MATERIALS	11. Material A	20	5
	12. Material B	20	5
	13. Packaging materials	20	5
VII. ADMINISTRATION	14. Order handling	33	3
	15. Credit and collections	20	2
Total	Cost accounted for		48.5[a]

[a] Fifteen activities—out of many hundreds—thus account for 50 cents of each consumer dollar.

without, apparently, getting paid. And the high cost of order handling and credit (items 14 and 15) also pointed to something basically wrong in the company's distribution system.

Packaging materials – item 13 – came as a real shock. Here was a major cost element that had not been seen at all. While other materials were bought by the purchasing agent, packaging materials had been left to the package designers in marketing. And they, obviously, had not given attention to the cost of packaging, nor, as the charges for handling finished goods showed, to packages designed for cheap and easy transportation, loading and storage.

In some important areas this analysis made possible immediate action. For example:

A transportation study was obviously in order. It reduced total transportation costs by almost one-third, and almost eliminated transportation between plants.

Warehousing and inventory costs – almost 10 per cent of the total – were drastically reduced. A small number of modern warehouses were found to be able to give faster service more cheaply than a large number of small and old-fashioned ones. Inventories in the hands of distributors were all but cut out as the warehouse could give overnight service.

Receivables were sharply cut, as were order handling and credit and collections. At the same time effectiveness of the sales effort was greatly increased. It was already known in the company – as a result of the analyses of the result areas – that while a dealer force of ten thousand individual retailers carried the company's products, the largest two thousand of these dealers accounted for something like 80 per cent of the company's sales, with the remaining eight thousand accounting for 80 per cent of the actual cost of supplying the market. Effective cost control therefore meant doing something about the three thousand smallest retailers who, each selling at most $3,000 worth of the company's products a year, accounted for no more than 5 or 6 per cent of total company sales. But studies triggered by this analysis and focused on the major cost points such as transportation, inventories, receivables and administration showed that these small dealers were responsible for almost 40 per cent of the costs in these areas. They accounted for the bulk of the receivables, i.e., were the ones the company had to finance. They also accounted for a disproportionate share of both transportation costs and order handling costs as they ordered only small quantities. And they, of course, *were* the credit-and-collections costs.

These small dealers were put on a cash-with-order basis. Salesmen stopped calling on them. Instead, they were solicited by mail; and only mail orders for minimum quantities were accepted from them, and shipped, with freight charged in full, from the warehouse nearest to them. Over three years this cut total costs of the delivered product by 9 per cent – as much as the total cost of manufacturing. Receivables, for instance, all but disappeared, as did the costs of credit and collection. But the purchases of the small retailers only dropped by one-third, or about 2 per cent of total sales. Total sales actually went up as the salesmen, no longer forced to spend one-third of their time calling on unproductive accounts, concentrated their energies and time where the sales opportunities were; that is, on the larger retailer.

But to treat each major cost point as a separate problem is still inadequate. An analysis of cost points will always bring out that costs constitute a system. Necessary efforts and their expenses can be taken at more than one place – though with very different results.

In Universal Products, for instance, low over-all costs may well have been achieved by keeping inventory on the high side. This might make manufacturing efficient – by enabling it, for instance, to schedule production at an even pace the year round; thus avoiding the cost of fluctuations and perhaps even the costs – fixed and operating – of a plant large enough to turn out peak demand. But higher inventories may also cost so much more than uneven production as to be sheer waste.

Only a study that looks upon the entire physical flow and storage of materials as one system (a study well within the capabilities of an operations researcher or a systems engineer) can tell whether and to what extent lower manufacturing costs compensate for higher inventory costs.

Similarly, a company might well use higher inventories, quick deliveries and, above all, a liberal credit and collection policy for the retailer as 'promotion', rather than promote its products heavily with the consumer. In respect to the small retail customer of Universal Products this was not productive, as the analysis shows. The small outlets did not produce sales commensurate to the investment in them. But what about the larger outlets? Maybe for best – and cheapest – promotion results they should be better serviced and financed.

For goods which the consumer himself picks off the shelves – packaged goods for instance – direct consumer promotion is obviously important, though not necessarily decisive. But a student going off to college and buying a portable typewriter depends heavily on the advice of the 'expert', the dealer or his salesman. As long as the consumer has heard the brand name before, he will accept the dealer's decision. Promoting the dealer – through higher dealer discounts, for example, or through financing him – may be the most effective and cheapest promotion for such goods. It may, for instance, explain in large part the tremendous success of a little-advertised German typewriter in the United States these last few years.

Each major cost point has to be seen therefore as a segment of the cost stream. Each proposed course of action on one cost point must be tested against the question: What will it do to the cost of work in other areas? There is no 'cheap' or 'efficient' manufacturing as such. There is only manufacturing that results in a cheap or efficient product or service to the customer. The relationship of costs to each other must be understood; 'sub-optimizing', which controls and reduces costs in one area at the expense of costs and effectiveness in other areas must be avoided. But it is highly desirable to make trade-offs; i.e., to be able to forgo apparent cost advantages in one area (to the point even of accepting higher costs) in order to obtain larger cost advantages in other areas, and thereby significantly lower total costs for the entire processes.*

THE COST CATEGORIES

Major cost points fall into four main categories:

1. *Productive costs* are the costs of efforts intended to provide the value the customer wants and is willing to pay for. True manufacturing costs belong here; and so do costs of promotion. The costs of knowledge-work and of money-work belong here, and so does the cost of selling. Packaging should be here in so far as it makes a product distinct.

---

* The much-publicized PERT and PERT/COST Systems (with PERT standing for Programme Evaluation and Review Techniques) are tools to work out both visually and mathematically such relations in a very complex system such as a major new missile or a space ship, especially for trade-offs both in respect to time and to costs.

2. *Support costs* provide no value by themselves, but cannot be avoided in the process. Transportation is a typical cost of this kind. The order-handling costs in administration belong in this category, as do inspection or personnel work, accounting, and so on. In an 'ideal theory' of business, these activities can be disregarded or treated as overhead. In the real world, they consume as much effort as friction consumes energy in real machines.

3. *Policing costs* are the costs of activities which do not aim at getting something done but at preventing the wrong things from happening. Any business needs early warning systems to report when a product is not selling according to expectations, for instance, or when the company's technology no longer gives it a competitive edge. And here belong also the costs of policing others, suppliers or distributors, for instance.

4. *Waste* is the cost of efforts that cannot produce results.

The costliest waste is 'not-doing'; machine down-time, for instance. Everybody waits till the repairman comes or till the new production run starts. Everybody waits till the ovens, after melting one aluminium alloy, have cooled sufficiently to be cleaned and prepared for the melt of another, different alloy. Not-doing is the oil-tanker running empty from the refinery on the U.S. East Coast back to the Arabian Gulf, or the equally specialized banana boat returning empty from Rotterdam to Ecuador. The 150-seat jet plane sitting in the hangar or flying with only fifteen paying customers; or the freighter spending five days in port loading or unloading – when it only earns at sea carrying cargo – all these are not-doing.

These are not moral terms but economic ones. Admittedly, they fall far short of scientific precision. But some such classification that distinguishes the major cost points by relating them to results is essential. For each classification needs different analysis and requires a different approach to controlling costs.

In analysing *productive costs* the proper question is: What is most effective? What produces the most results with the least input of effort and expense?

The concept of the cost of incremental acquisition described in Chapter 4 therefore applies here. Productive costs should be increased up to, but not beyond, the point at which the unit of incremental acquisition for an additional unit of input falls sharply.

What this means is that productive costs are not controllable as 'costs' at all. They are controlled through the concentration of resources on opportunities. They require 'result control' rather than 'cost control'.

Their measurement is therefore always the productivity of the resources employed. Productive costs need to be measured in terms of the results obtained by the three key resources of men, time and money. What cost control adds to the previous analysis of result areas and of the allocation of resources to them are productivity measurements: output and profit per dollar of pay-roll as a cost measurement of the productivity of people; output and profit per man-hour and per machine-hour as a cost measurement of the productivity of time; and output and profit per dollar of total money at work as the cost measurement of the productivity of capital.* Concentrating resources on opportunities is the only effective way to control productive costs.

Support costs always have to prove first that they are needed at all. One always asks: 'How much do we stand to lose if we do nothing?' And if the answer is: 'Less than the minimum cost of support,' then it is better to run the risk of an occasional loss and save the support costs. One should never spend more than 99 cents to gain a dollar; and where the gain is only possible – even where it is probable – spending 99 cents for it is too much.

A good example of how *not* to handle support costs is the story, a few pages back, of the manner in which Universal Products handled its distribution costs. By putting the three thousand smallest of its retailers on a mail-order cash basis, it cut costs sharply. But it still maintained costs that were larger than any possible return. For even on a mail-order cash basis, a small retailer is expensive; the total cost of maintaining those outlets certainly amounted to more than the possible profit from their sales. Dropping these submarginal outlets altogether would probably not even have cost any sales – bigger orders from the profitable large retailers would, in all probability, have made up the loss fast enough.

If support costs cannot be cut out altogether, one asks: 'What is the least cost and effort that will get by?'

---

* These should be projected on 'value-added' figures of output rather than on gross sales figures. Where raw materials utilization is an important element, a raw-materials productivity figure might be added which shows sales and profits per unit of material.

In support costs this 'least-effort' principle always leads to a redesign and reorganization of activities.

The physical handling and movement of things in manufacturing and distributing businesses may be the heaviest support cost. Even where there are no physical goods to be moved – that is, in financial and service businesses – the cost of physical movement and handling, of storage, of mailing, etc., of such things as documents, policies, cheques, bills, etc., is a large cost centre. Yet few businesses have the remotest idea of the cost of physical handling and movement. Many do not even know their freight bill, which, after all, is a straight, out-of-pocket cash payment.

To control transportation costs, the entire flow of materials should be seen as both a physical and economic system in which the greatest amount of physical performance is to be given with the least economic effort. The entire job – from the moment things come off the machine through crating, packaging, labelling, shipping, warehousing, storage, and so on, right through to the final destination of the merchandise in the customer's home or place of business – has to be seen and analysed as one integrated process.

It has to be accomplished at the least possible cost and give the greatest economic value to all parties – manufacturer, wholesaler, retailer and customer.

This, needless to say, cannot be done overnight. We do have, however, the tools today to do the job – in the management sciences above all – and have achieved remarkable results wherever we have really gone to work.

The best thing to do with *policing* costs is not to police. The question is again: 'Are we likely to lose more than it costs us to police?' If the answer is 'No,' it is better not to police. If this cannot be done, the least-effort principle applies. It usually consists in policing and preventing activities by means of a small but statistically valid sample, rather than through inspecting and monitoring every single event or transaction.

Inventory controls or quality controls are already handled this way in a good many businesses. Acceptable limits of non-performance are set. How poor can customer acceptance of the product, minimum fulfilment of delivery promises, or of manufacturing schedules be before it endangers desired business results ? The control can then be carried out through a small sample – which, of course, sharply cuts work and costs.

Perhaps the most elegant way of handling policing costs through a statistical method using a small sample is to find an activity which has to be done anyhow and which yet controls and audits a great many areas that otherwise would have to be policed.

One of the major shipping lines, for instance, uses the handling of complaints as the quality control for its entire freight operation, for its piers and terminals, and for the treatment of passengers.

Claims arise when goods are damaged, delivered late, delivered to the wrong address, etc. They may also arise from injuries to passengers or from damage to their belongings. If the goal were to settle claims at lowest cost they would be put on a simple, statistical basis. Ninety-five per cent of all claims would then require no investigation.

In this shipping line, however, claims investigation is used as the quality control for all operating activities. The theory (amply confirmed by subsequent experience) was that shortcomings in the handling of freight or passengers anywhere on the line show up as claims fairly fast. Investigating every claim therefore gives 100 per cent control of all operating failures. Yet all the claims together are still a smaller sample than would be needed for statistical quality control of the entire operation.

This example also shows that truly effective control of policing costs requires study and hard, sustained work. The ordinary cost-control approach will not work here. On the contrary it may well push up these costs. The first thing management in a cost-reduction drive tends to do is to police more and to prevent more.

The High Cost of Not-doing

Waste rarely needs to be analysed. It is usually quite clear that this or that cost cannot produce results; whether we can do anything about it, is another question.

But waste is often hard to find. The costs of not-doing tend to be hidden in the figures.

This is of course not true for not-doing as blatant as the tanker returning in ballast or the jet plane flying empty. But for many years the shipping companies did not realize that their main costs were costs of idle time in port rather than costs of carrying goods at sea. The port time was just 'overhead'. As a result the emphasis in ship design and management was on a fast trip at low operating costs at sea. But cutting down already low seagoing costs resulted in making port costs even higher, loading and unloading even slower, turn-around time in port even longer.

Such attempts to come to grips with the costs of not-doing as the 'minimum economical run' for a certain model (that is, the number of pieces – or of hours – in a run required for adequate machine utilization) are on the whole inadequate. They are still figures for doing rather than for not-doing. They rarely include the often high price for interruption of work and diminution of productivity incumbent upon any shift from one model or variety to another: the cooling and cleaning of the melting ovens for aluminium alloys, for instance, during which the whole expensive rolling-mill equipment and all the people employed wait idly. They also rarely include equipment-utilization differentials.

Thus one particular aluminium alloy may utilize the *rolling* equipment as well as another one, but utilize practically none of the *finishing* equipment. Because of that, accounting may set the cost of the alloy 30 per cent lower – and it will be priced accordingly. Yet the finishing equipment has nothing to do while this particular alloy is being rolled. Though the equipment stands idle, however, its costs go on; and the finishing department is where the bulk of the people and therefore the heaviest costs are found. The normally available figures would not reveal this.

Waste runs high in any business. Man, after all, is not very efficient. Special efforts to find waste are therefore always necessary.

One indication that the costs of not-doing are high is usually furnished by the accounting figures themselves. Whenever the 'allocated manufacturing expenses', or their equivalent, run to one-third or more of total manufacturing cost, I suspect high, hidden waste costs. Another warning signal is sharp discrepancy between the cost-share of a product in the accounting figures and its *share of the cost burden* as calculated on the basis of the transactions it is responsible for.

But the best way to find waste is to look for it, and especially to ask: Where are we spending time, money and people for not-doing and on producing non-results?

There is only one sensible thing to do with waste-creating activities: drop them.

Sometimes this requires little effort; as in the illustration above where three thousand small retailers, out of a total ten thousand or so, could be dropped, thus eliminating a high cost of doing nothing (in this case selling nothing).

But many wasteful activities are hard to get rid of. It sometimes requires a major redesign of a whole business; more often it requires basic changes in operating practices, in equipment, in policies.

To fill the empty airplane seats with paying customers might, for instance, require a redesign of routes or of tariff structures, or major promotional efforts to attract a different and new class of customers. Eliminating machine down-time might require adoption of preventive maintenance or of a new and different scheduling system and of new inventory practices. Cutting wasteful time of freighters in port might require redesign of the general-cargo freighter into a seagoing materials-handling plant, and so on.

Such efforts, however, are totally outside of the conventional approach to cost control and cost cutting. They require major, prolonged efforts; indeed, a good deal of the most expensive waste is typically found in 'restraints' on a business – and as such is a major potential that needs to be converted into an opportunity.

Most cost cutting, let alone the across-the-board cut, does not even touch waste. Yet, in every business waste is a real cost centre.

The management of costs requires the same kind of systematic, organized approach as has been developed in earlier chapters for the management of result areas and resources. The conclusion from the analysis of the cost streams – what to tackle, where to go to work, what to aim at – should become part of the over-all understanding of the business and of the comprehensive programme for making it fully effective.

6

The Customer Is the Business

The analysis of the business; its result areas, its revenues, its resources allocation and leadership position, its cost centres and cost structure, answers the question: *How* are we doing? But how do we know whether we are doing the right things? What, in other words, is our business – and what should it be? This question calls for a different analysis, an analysis that looks at the business from the outside.

Business is a process which converts a resource, distinct knowledge, into a contribution of economic value in the market place. The purpose of a business* is to create a customer. The purpose is to provide something for which an independent outsider, who can choose not to buy, is willing to exchange his purchasing power. And knowledge alone (excepting only the case of the complete monopoly) gives the products of any business that leadership position on which success and survival ultimately depend.

From the inside it is not easy to find out what a business gets paid for. Organized attempts to look at one's own business from the outside are needed.

As experienced a company as Radio Corporation of America (RCA) was convinced that the consumer would recognize and accept the RCA trademark on refrigerators and ranges when it entered the kitchen appliance business in the 'forties. RCA is, of course, one of the best-known consumer trademarks for radios and television sets. To a manufacturer these are as much 'appliances' as are kitchen ranges. For the consumer they are an entirely different category of goods, carrying different value connotations. Trademark acceptance in the market did not carry over from radios to ranges and RCA had to withdraw from the kitchen appliance business. It is quite possible – indeed, likely – that the RCA trademark would have carried customer acceptance for tape recorders and photographic cameras. To a manufacturer, however, radios and cameras are entirely different goods.

* To repeat something first said a decade ago, in my *Practice of Management* (New York: Harper & Row, 1954; and London: William Heinemann, 1954).

There are scores of similar examples. What to the manufacturer is one market or one category of products is to the customer often a number of unrelated markets and a number of different satisfactions and values.

People inside a business can rarely be expected to recognize their own distinct knowledge; they take it for granted. What one knows how to do, by and large, comes easy. As a result the people in the business tend to assume, unthinkingly, that there is nothing to their knowledge or special ability, indeed that everybody else must have it too. What looms large on their horizon are the things they find hard – that is, the things they are not particularly good at.

A major, highly diversified company making chemical, pharmaceutical and cosmetic specialties has great ability in finding, developing and holding together a group of highly individualistic, aggressive division heads. Each is a professional manager, up from the ranks. Yet each runs his division as if it were his own business. Each is jealous of any encroachment by one of the other divisions – indeed, considers some of them direct and dangerous competitors. Yet all work closely with a small but able top management group and they work with each other in a harmonious team on all matters concerning the entire company. Problems that plague every other company of this kind – where, for instance, no division head will voluntarily give up one of his good people to another division – do not exist for these men. Yet nobody has been able to convince the management group in the company that they are doing something remarkable.

Sears Roebuck is a good example here too – precisely because few companies in the United States have so carefully analysed themselves.

To the outsider it seems obvious that Sears' most important knowledge area is buying: the design of the right merchandise; the selection of the right assortment; the selection of the source from which to buy – and if necessary, manufacturing either in a wholly-owned plant or in partnership. Not much less important is selection of store location, architecture and design. These, however, are not the knowledge areas which Sears people themselves stress. Both inside their own group and when talking to the public, they stress selling. The outside observer is hard put, however, to see anything distinctive in Sears selling – it does not differ noticeably from every other mass-merchant's selling. But the hero of the Sears sagas is always a store manager. And far more of the top jobs seem to go to people who came up as store managers than go to people with buying or store-planning backgrounds.

I am not saying that the people inside a business are bound to be wrong in their appraisal of what the business does and what it gets paid for. But they cannot take for granted that they are right. The least they can do is to test their judgement.

MARKET REALITIES

All this is hardly news for businessmen any more. For a decade now the 'marketing view' has been widely publicized. It has even acquired a fancy name: The Total Marketing Approach.

Not everything that goes by that name deserves it. 'Marketing' has become a fashionable term. But a gravedigger remains a gravedigger even when called a 'mortician' – only the cost of the burial goes up. Many a sales manager has been renamed 'marketing vice-president' – and all that happened was that costs and salaries went up.

A good deal of what is called 'marketing' today is at best organized, systematic selling in which the major jobs – from sales forecasting to warehousing and advertising – are brought together and co-ordinated. This is all to the good. But its starting point is still *our* products, *our* customers, *our* technology. The starting point is still the inside.

Yet there have been enough serious efforts for us to know what we mean by the marketing analysis of a business, and how one goes about it.

Here, first, are the marketing realities that are most likely to be encountered:

1. What the people in the business think they know about customer and market is more likely to be wrong than right. There is only one person who really knows: the customer. Only by asking the customer, by watching him, by trying to understand his behaviour can one find out who he is, what he does, how he buys, how he uses what he buys, what he expects, what he values, and so on.

2. The customer rarely buys what the business thinks it sells

him. One reason for this is, of course, that nobody pays for a 'product'. What is paid for is satisfactions. But nobody can make or supply satisfactions as such – at best, only the means to attaining them can be sold and delivered.

Every few years this axiom is rediscovered by a newcomer to the advertising business who becomes an overnight sensation on Madison Avenue. For a few months he brushes aside what the company's executives tell him about the product and its virtues, and instead turns to the customer and, in effect, asks him: 'And what do you look for? Maybe this product has it.' The formula has never failed – not since it was used, many years ago, to promote an automobile with the slogan, 'Ask the Man Who Owns One'; that is, with the promise of customer satisfaction. But it is so difficult for the people who make a product to accept that what they make and sell is the vehicle for customer satisfaction, rather than customer satisfaction itself, that the lesson is always immediately forgotten, until the next Madison Avenue sensation rediscovers it.

3. A corollary is that the goods or services which the manufacturer sees as direct competitors rarely adequately define what and whom he is really competing with. They cover both too much and too little.

Luxury cars – the Rolls-Royce and the Cadillac, for instance – are obviously not in real competition with low-priced automobiles. However excellent Rolls-Royce and Cadillac may be as transportation, they are mainly being bought for the prestige satisfaction they give.

Because the customer buys satisfaction, all goods and services compete intensively with goods and services that look quite different, seem to serve entirely different functions, are made, distributed, sold differently – but are alternative means for the customer to obtain the same satisfaction.

That the Cadillac competes for the customer's money with mink coats, jewellery, the ski-ing vacation in the luxury resort, and other prestige satisfactions, is an example – and one of the few both the general public and the businessman understand.

But the manufacturer of bowling equipment also does not, primarily, compete with the other manufacturers of bowling equipment. He makes physical equipment. But the customer buys an activity. He buys something to do rather than something to have. The competition is therefore all the other activities that compete for the rapidly growing 'discretionary time' of an affluent, urban population – boating and lawn care, for instance, but also the continuing postgraduate education of already highly schooled adults (which has been the true growth industry in the United States these last twenty years). That the bowling equipment makers were first in realizing the potential and growth of the discretionary-time market, first to promote a new family activity, explains their tremendous success in the 'fifties. That they, apparently, defined competition as other bowling equipment makers rather than as all suppliers of activity-satisfactions is in large part responsible for the abrupt decline of their fortunes in the 'sixties. They apparently had not even realized that other activities were invading the discretionary-time market; and they had not given thought to developing a successor-activity to a product that, in the activities market, was clearly becoming yesterday's product.

Even the direct competitors are, however, often overlooked. The big chemical companies, for instance, despite their careful industry intelligence, are capable of acting as if there were no competitors to worry about.

When in the early 'fifties the first of the volume plastics, polyethylene, established itself in the market, every major chemical company in America saw its tremendous growth potential. Everyone, it seems, arrived at about the same, almost unbelievable, growth forecast. But no one, it seems, realized that what was so obvious to him might not be totally invisible to the other chemical companies. Every major chemical company seems to have based its expansion plans in polyethylene on the assumption that no one else would expand capacity. Demand for polyethylene actually grew faster than even the almost incredible forecasts of that time anticipated. But because everybody expanded on the assumption that his new plants would get the entire new business, there is such over-capacity now that the price has collapsed and the plants are half-empty.

4. Another important corollary is that what the producer or supplier thinks the most important feature of a product to be – what they mean when they speak of its 'quality' – may well be

relatively unimportant to the customer. It is likely to be what is hard, difficult and expensive to make. But the customer is not moved in the least by the manufacturer's troubles. His only question is – and should be: 'What does this do for *me*?'

How difficult this is for businessmen to grasp, let alone to accept, the advertisements prove. One after the other stresses how complicated, how laborious, it is to make this or that product. 'Our engineers had to suspend the Laws of Nature to make this possible' is a constant theme. If this makes any impression on the customer, it is likely to be the opposite of the intended one: 'If this is so hard to make right,' he will say, 'it probably doesn't work.'

5. The customers have to be assumed to be rational. But their rationality is not necessarily that of the manufacturer; it is that of their own situation.

To assume – as has lately become fashionable – that customers are irrational is as dangerous a mistake as it is to assume that the customer's rationality is the same as that of the manufacturer or supplier – or that it should be.

A lot of pseudo-psychological nonsense has been spouted because the American housewife behaves as a different person when buying her groceries and when buying her lipstick. As the weekly food-buyer for the family, she tends to be highly price-conscious; she deserts the most familiar brand as soon as another offers a 'five-cents-off' special. Of course. She buys food as a 'professional', as the general home manager. But who would want to be married to a woman who buys lipstick the same way? Not to use the same criterion in what are two entirely different roles – and yet both real, rather than make-believe – is the only possible behaviour for a rational person.

It is the manufacturer's or supplier's job to find out why the customer behaves in what seems to be an irrational manner. It is his job either to adapt himself to the customer's rationality or to try to change it. But he must first understand and respect it.

6. No single product or company is very important to the market. Even the most expensive and most wanted product is just a small part of a whole array of available products, services, satisfactions. It is at most of minor interest to the customer, if he thinks of it at all. And the customer cares just as little for any one company or any one industry. There is no social security in the market, no seniority, no old-age disability pensions. The market is a harsh

employer who will dismiss even the most faithful servant without a penny of severance pay. The sudden disintegration of a big company would greatly upset employees and suppliers, banks, labour unions, plant-cities and governments. But it would hardly cause a ripple in the market.

For the businessman this is hard to swallow. What one does and produces is inevitably important to oneself. The businessman must see his company and its products as the centre. The customer does not, as a rule, see them at all.

How many housewives have ever discussed the whiteness of their laundry over the back fence? Of all possible topics of housewifely conversation, this surely ranks close to the bottom. Yet not only do advertisements play that theme over and over again, but soap company executives all believe that how well their soap washes is a matter of major concern, continuing interest and constant comparison to housewives – for the simple reason that it is, of course, a matter of real concern and interest to them (and should be).

7. All the statements so far imply that we know who the customer is. However, a marketing analysis has to be based on the assumption that a business normally does not know but needs to find out.

Not 'who pays' but 'who determines the buying decision' is the 'customer'.

The customer for the pharmaceutical industry used to be the druggist who compounded medicines either according to a doctor's prescription or according to his own formula. Today the determining buying decision for prescription drugs clearly lies with the physician. But is the patient purely passive – just the man who pays the bill for whatever the physician buys for him? Or is the patient – or at least the public – a major customer, what with all the interest in, and publicity for, the wonder drugs? Has the druggist lost completely his former customer status? The drug companies clearly do not agree in their answers to these questions; yet a different answer leads to very different measures.

The minimum number of customers with decisive impact on the buying decision is always two: the ultimate buyer and the distributive channel.

A manufacturer of processed canned foods, for instance, has two main customers: the housewife and the grocery store.

Unless the grocer gives his products adequate shelf space, they cannot be bought by the housewife. It is self-deception on the part of the manufacturer to believe that the housewife will be so loyal to his brand that she would rather shop elsewhere than buy another well-known brand she finds prominently displayed on the shelves.

Which of these two, ultimate buyer or distributive channel, is the more important customer is often impossible to determine. There is, for instance, a good deal of evidence that national advertising, though ostensibly directed at the consumer, is most effective with the retailer, is indeed the best way to move him to promote a brand. But there is also plenty of evidence – contrary to all that is said about 'hidden persuaders' – that distributors, no matter how powerfully supported by advertising, cannot sell a product that the consumer for whatever reason does not accept.

Who is the customer tends to be more complex and more difficult to determine for industrial than for consumer goods. Who is the ultimate consumer and who is the distributive channel for the manufacturer of power equipment for machinery: the purchasing agent of the machinery manufacturer who lets the contract; or the engineer who sets the specifications? The buyer of the completed machine? While the latter is usually without power to decide from which maker the parts of the machine (e.g., the motor starter and the motor controls) should come, he almost always has power to veto any given supplier. All three – if not many more – are customers.

Each class of customers has different needs, wants, habits, expectations, value concepts, and so on. Yet each has to be sufficiently satisfied at least not to veto a purchase.

8. But what if no identifiable customer can be found for a business or an industry? A great many businesses have no one person or group of persons who could be called their customer.

Who, for example, is the customer of a major glass company which makes everything as long as it is glass? It may sell to everybody – from the buyer of automobile instrument-board lights to the collector of expensive hand-blown vases. It has no one customer, no one particular want to satisfy, no one particular value expectation to meet.

Similarly, in buying paper for a package, the printer, the

packaging designer, the packaging converter, the customer's advertising agency, and the customer's sales and design people, all can – and do – decide what paper not to buy. And yet none of them makes the buying decision itself. None of these people buys paper as such. The decision is made indirectly, through deciding on shape, cost, carrying capacity of the package, graphic appearance, and so on. Who is actually the customer?

There are two large and important groups of industries in which it is difficult and sometimes impossible to identify the customer: materials industries and end-use supply (or equipment) makers.

Materials industries are organized around the exploitation of one raw material, such as petroleum or copper; or around one process, such as the glassmaker, the steel mill, or the paper mill. Their products are of necessity material-determined rather than market-determined. The end-use industries, such as a manufacturer of adhesives – starches, bonding materials, glues, and so on – have no one process or material to exploit. Adhesives can be made from vegetable matter such as corn or potatoes, from animal fats, and from synthetic polymers furnished by the petrochemical industry. But there is still no easily identifiable, no distinct customer. Adhesives are used in almost every industrial process. But to say – as one would have to say about the steel mill or the adhesives plant – that everyone is his customer, is to say that no one is an identifiable customer.

The answer is not, however, that these businesses cannot be subjected to a marketing analysis. Rather, markets or end-uses, instead of customers, are the starting point for this analysis in materials and end-use industries.

Materials businesses – steel or copper, for instance – can usually be understood best in terms of markets. It is meaningful to say, for instance, that a certain percentage of all copper products go into the construction market – though they go to such a multitude of different customers and for such a variety of end-uses that these two dimensions may well defy analysis. It is meaningful to say that the adhesives all serve one end-use: to hold together the surfaces of different materials, though neither customer analysis nor market analysis may make much sense.

The view from outside has three dimensions rather than one. It asks not only 'Who buys?' but 'Where is it bought?' and 'What is it being bought for ?' *Every business can thus be defined as serving either customers, or markets, or end-uses.* Which of the three, however, is the appropriate dimension for a given business cannot be answered without study. Every marketing analysis of a business therefore should work through all three dimensions to find the one that fits best. This, by the way, is why the phrase 'customers, markets, end-uses' has appeared so often in the preceding chapters.

Again and again one finds (1) that a dimension the people in the business consider quite inappropriate – customers or end-uses in a paper company, for instance – is actually highly important; and (2) that superimposing the findings from the analysis of one of these dimensions on another one – e.g., analysis of a paper company in terms of paper end-uses, paper markets, and paper customers – yields powerful and productive insights.

Even where there is a clearly identifiable customer, one does well to examine the business also in relation to its markets or the end-uses of its products or services. This is the only way one can be sure of defining adequately what satisfaction it serves, for whom and how. It is often the only way to determine on what developments and factors its future will depend.

These market realities lead to one conclusion: the most *important* questions about a business are those that try to penetrate the real world of the consumer, the world in which the manufacturer and his products barely exist.

How to See the Unexpected

All the standard questions of a market study should, of course, be asked: Who is the customer? Where is the customer? How does he buy? What does he consider value? What purposes of the customer do our products satisfy? What role in the customer's life and work does our particular product play? How important is it to him? Under what circumstances – age, for instance, or structure of the family – is this purpose most important to the customer? Under what circumstances is it least important to him? Who are the direct and the indirect competitors? What are they doing? What might they be doing tomorrow?

But the emphasis might be on different questions that are rarely asked. They are the questions that force us to see the unexpected.

1. Who is the non-customer, the man who does not buy our

products even though he is (or might be) in the market? And can we find out why he is a non-customer?

One illustration is the experience of a successful manufacturer and distributor of do-it-yourself home-repair and home-maintenance supplies and equipment. A market study brought out that his main customer was the newly married family with the first home of its own. It would be an eager customer for about five years and then gradually fade out. This seemed perfectly logical to the manufacturer. After all, these were the people who were most actively interested in the home. They had the energy to do manual work. And, having small children, they normally spent most of their evenings and weekends at home.

But when non-customers – families married longer than five years – were actually looked at, they were found to be a potentially excellent market. They were non-customers primarily because the company had chosen a distributive channel, especially the neighbouring hardware store, which was not easily accessible to them except Saturday morning. Saturday morning is not a good shopping time for men, once children, though still young, are past their infancy. Putting the merchandise into shopping centres (which remain open in the evenings when, increasingly, the whole family goes shopping together), and adding mail-selling directly to the home, more than doubled the manufacturer's sales. To be sure, a smaller percentage of the older homeowners buys, and the older family buys somewhat less per year. But at any one time there are many more people who have owned a home for five years or longer than there are new owners. A smaller percentage of the older age group still yields a bigger business than a higher share of the younger market.

2. Equally important may be the question: What does the customer buy altogether? What does he do with his money and with his time?

Normally companies want to know what share of the customer's total spending – his disposable income, his discretionary income or his discretionary time* – goes on their products, and whether

---

* Which mean respectively: cash remaining after taxes and other compulsory deductions from the pay cheque; cash available after 'necessities' have been paid for; time available and not needed to make a living and to get the necessary rest, i.e., time available for leisure, recreation, education, and so on.

the share is going up or down. This is important, of course. But to have some idea how the customer disposes of all his money and time may tell a good deal more.

Asking this question brought out, for instance, that neither price nor quality was the determinant of purchasing decisions for the products of a major construction materials company. What determined purchase was whether it could be accounted for as capital investment or as operating expense. What made the purchase possible for one group of potential customers, especially public bodies – namely, that the purchase appeared as an operating expense in their books – made it difficult for the other group, the private businesses, for whom a capital-investment appears as an asset while operating expenses interfere with profit figures in the books. The same products had to be 'packaged' differently for the two kinds of customers: Public bodies got a ten-year 'rental' in which the initial investment was paid off as part of an annual rental charge; private businesses were offered a capital-asset at a price which included ten years' free maintenance.

This leads in turn to two questions that are not asked in the ordinary market survey or customer study:

3. What do customers – and non-customers – buy from others? And what value do these purchases have for them? What satisfactions do they give? Do they, indeed, actually or potentially compete with the satisfactions our products or services are offering? Or do they give satisfactions our products or services – or products or services we could render – could provide too, perhaps even better?

What this question might unearth are the value preferences of the market. How important in his life is the satisfaction the customer obtains from us? Is the importance likely to grow or to diminish? And in what areas of satisfaction does he have new or inadequately satisfied wants?

4. This is, of course, very close to the crucial question: What product or service would fulfil the satisfaction areas of real importance – both those we now serve and those we might serve?

The most imaginative illustration I know is that of a South American soft drink bottler who, while doing well, noticed that he was rapidly approaching market saturation. He thereupon asked himself: 'What new product would, in the present stage of our economy, most nearly resemble the satisfaction which soft drinks offered to the masses fifty years ago?' His answer was paperback books. The population, while still very poor, had become literate in the meantime. Yet books in South America are available only in a few stores in the large cities and then at prices which even the middle-class can hardly afford. Paperback books, this man concluded, are, for today's population, precisely the small luxury which soft drinks were for the barefoot Indians half a century back. And in respect to merchandising, mass-distribution, mass-display and the need rapidly to return unsold merchandise, paperback books are almost exactly like bottled soft drinks. What the man learned about his business, in other words, is that it was not 'soft drinks'; it was 'mass-merchandising'.

Four additional areas demand investigation.

First: What would enable the customers to do without our product or services? What would force them to do without? On what in the customer's world – economy, business, market – do we, in other words, depend? Is it economics? Is it such trends as the constant shifts from goods into services, and from low price into high convenience in an affluent society? What is the outlook? And are we geared to take advantage of the factors favourable to us?

Second: What are the meaningful aggregates in the customer's mind and in his economy? What makes them aggregates?

Two examples will explain this question:

When the automatic dishwasher was first developed, the makers went to great trouble and expense to make this new kitchen appliance look just like the clothes washer – an appliance the housewife had enthusiastically accepted and was thoroughly familiar with. Since technically the two appliances are quite different, to make them look alike – especially in out-side dimensions – was no mean achievement. Yet the main reason why the dishwasher has – so far – been a disappoint-ment to its manufacturers is the ingenuity that went into mak-ing it look exactly like its older cousin, the clothes washer. For while it looks alike, it costs twice as much. To the housewife who is no engineer – and sees no reason why she should be one – this makes no sense. If something has been made to look exactly like the automatic clothes washer, why then should it cost twice as much? In other words, the manufacturers put the automatic dishwasher into a set of aggregrates in which it created price expectations it could not meet. It is likely that the dishwasher would have done much better had it looked so different from the traditional kitchen appliances as to stand out clearly as something new, as something not belonging in this familiar aggregate: kitchen appliances.

Another example is the totally different experience Sears Roebuck has had with two kinds of insurance. When it introduced, in the 'thirties, automobile insurance as something sold through its retail stores – like any other merchandise – it was exceedingly successful. The Sears-owned insurance company rapidly became the second largest underwriter of automobile insurance in the United States. When, twenty years later, it introduced life insurance, it met with considerable customer resistance and has not yet been able to repeat its earlier automobile insurance success. To the customer, automobile insurance is essentially a product, an automobile accessory, and as much a part of the car as brakes or steering-wheel. But life insurance is something different; it is finance rather than merchandise. It simply does not belong to the same aggregate as automobile insurance – that both have the word 'insurance' in their name does not make them sufficiently alike.

Another case of mistaken aggregation by the manufacturer had a happier ending.

A manufacturer of garden products introduced a line for the rose grower – a special fertilizer, pesticide, and so on. A leading supplier, he expected the new line to be rapidly accepted. Almost every home gardener has roses and wants to take care of them. As 'rose products' the new line was a failure. But as products for the care of flowers and shrubs in general, they began to sell well in a few places – even though the manufacturer in all his instructions stressed their exclusive application to roses. When the manufacturer accepted the customer's verdict and offered the products for all flowers and shrubs, the line, which he was ready to give up as a failure, suddenly came to life. 'Rose grower' clearly means 'somebody else' to the suburban home owner.

'Aggregates,' to use the terms of the psychologist, are 'configurations'. Their reality is in the eye of the beholder. They depend not on definition but on perception. The perceptions, and with them the aggregates of the manufacturer and of the customer, must be different; for they have different experiences and look for different things. Yet it is the customer's perception of aggregates that matters, that decides what he buys, when he buys, and whether he buys.

Another searchlight on the unexpected is the third question: Who are our non-competitors – and why?

There is nothing that changes faster than industry structures. Yet few things appear to executives so much like a law of nature as the industry structure of the moment. The present membership of the electrical industry association or of the Retail Grocers Institute is considered 'the industry'. Yet again and again total newcomers are suddenly the most effective competitors – especially when they offer the customer a basically different means of satisfying the same want. In no time, industry structure – yesterday seemingly so solid – is fragmented. Yet the new one, as it stabilizes after a time, is again taken for the ultimate.

Here are two examples:

The manufacturers of printing presses paid apparently no attention to the new processes for office reproduction that began to come on the market after World War II. These were not 'printing'; and the equipment for the processes was not being sold to 'printers'. One of the large printing-press manufacturers was offered several reproduction processes by the inventors and turned them down without any study. It was not until a large part of the printer's traditional work was being done by their former customers themselves on office reproduction equipment that the printing industry woke up to the fact that a competitor had appeared who was far more dangerous than another printing-press maker could have been.

Similarly, the fertilizer industry in the United States considered itself a 'chemical business'. The questions – Who are the non-competitors? Are they likely to remain non-competitors? – would at once have brought out that there is no reason why the petroleum companies are not in the fertilizer business. They furnish the most important raw material: ammonia (which is a by-product of natural gas). They are experts in mass distribution and have representation in the smallest hamlet in the country. And it was increasingly clear, in the late 'fifties, that the petroleum companies needed additional products for their huge and expensive distribution system. Yet even when one of the big American companies went into the fertilizer field in Europe, the U.S. fertilizer companies were convinced that it couldn't happen at home – until they woke up one fine day to find that the mixed-fertilizer business in the United States was being taken over by the petroleum industry.

The question: Who is our non-competitor? logically leads to the fourth question: Whose non-competitor are we? Where are there opportunities we neither see nor exploit – because we do not consider them part of our industry at all?

UNDERSTANDING THE CUSTOMER

Finally, one should always ask the question: What in the customer's behaviour appears to me totally irrational? And what therefore is it in *his* reality that I fail to see?

I have yet to find a consumer-goods manufacturer, for instance, who understands why every important retailer will – indeed, must – insist on having a private brand of his own. The more successful the retailer is in selling national (i.e., manufacturer's) brands, the more will he insist on carrying and promoting his own. Manufacturers ascribe this insistence to the retailer's shortsighted concern with profit margins instead of with total profit-dollars. Yet retailers usually admit that the higher profit margin of the private brand is eaten up by higher inventory costs and by the cost of goods left over which, being the retailer's own, cannot be returned. This only confirms the manufacturer in his belief that the retailer is irrational.

Actually, the retailer is perfectly rational in fearing that complete dependence on national brands will endanger him, no matter how much profit he makes on them. Why should anyone want to come to his store if all he sees and gets there are the same nationally advertised and nationally sold brands he can buy every place else for the same price and in the same quality? A store whose reputation rests exclusively on the brand names everybody else can carry has no reputation or identity at all. All it has is an address.

Attempting to understand seemingly irrational customer behaviour forces the manufacturer to adopt the marketing view rather than merely talk about it. Moreover, it forces the manufacturer to take action according to the logic of the market rather than according to the logic of the supplier. He must adapt himself to the customer's behaviour if he cannot turn it to his advantage. Or he has to embark on the more difficult job of changing the customer's habits and vision.

The retailer's desire for a private brand to establish his store's identity is in the retailer's own best interest. The manufacturer had therefore better adapt to it, and if possible, turn it to his own advantage. The dominant supplier in any given product range might himself become the supplier of the private brand too.

On the other hand, the buying practices of the large American electric power companies for large generating equipment – turbines, for instance – were, while rational, detrimental to the best long-term interests of manufacturers and power companies alike. They resulted in unnecessarily expensive equipment. Traditionally each generating station is designed as a completely separate project; and the power company's design engineer tries to put special features into every turbine and every generator. But the two large American turbine manufacturers – General Electric and Westinghouse – have such volume that only mass-production methods can handle it. Hence these individual touches for each turbine cause heavy additional costs. At the same time, they are unnecessary today; for practically every performance configuration can be obtained by putting standardized parts together.

In addition, power companies – rationally from their point of view – order heavy equipment not when they know they will need it, but when long-term interest rates are low. Every five years or so, there is thus a spate of rush orders. And two to three years later the turbine plants are overcrowded and run on three shifts in a desperate attempt to finish what was already overdue in most cases when it was first ordered. Few things, however, are as expensive as an overcrowded plant in which men, half-finished work, and equipment get in each other's way.

The equipment manufacturers have thus far tackled the. first part of the problem. In a long educational campaign they have been trying to get across that the power company could save a great deal of money if it were to specify performance of the equipment rather than its own detailed design. Apparently, they have made considerable progress. The second part of the job – the interest-rate determination of orders – has not been tackled yet, to my knowledge. (It should be possible to solve it, though. Interest rates, after all, are cyclical. If the equipment companies were to take on themselves the differential between the going rate at the time of contract and the lowest rate within the next five-year period, they would, at most, risk something like 10 per cent; for they could re-finance at the lower rate within five years. And the penalty for the feast-and-famine method of production imposed by the traditional pattern is likely to be a good deal higher.)

Wherever a manufacturer tries to impose what he considers rational on an apparent irrationality which turns out to be in the best interest of the customer, he is likely to lose the customer. At least, the customer will resent his attempt as a gross abuse of economic power – which it is. For behaviour, however, that is contrary to the customer's own best interests, the manufacturer in the end pays a heavy price.

The American pharmaceutical industry may soon become living proof of this. The typical doctor's preference for a branded drug over a generic one is rational enough. Modern pharmacology and biochemistry are way beyond most doctors, especially the older ones. How to combine several modern drugs in one prescription is far too complex for a busy practitioner ever to learn. He therefore prefers to depend on the manufacturer. That the doctor does not greatly care what medicines cost is also rational. After all, health insurance pays for it in most cases – and the patient therefore is unlikely to appreciate the doctor's efforts to save him money. There is thus a strong case for the brand. It may be the only way in which the average physician can acquire the necessary competence in using the new, highly potent drugs.

But it was the pharmaceutical companies' job to make this rationality of their distributive channel redound to the benefit of the ultimate consumer, the patient. Instead, they resigned themselves to the doctor's ignorance and made the patient pay for it through pricing branded compounds way above the same compounds sold as generic drugs under their scientific names. This predictably (and it *was* predicted by more than one good friend of the drug industry) will lead to punitive measures – which, as always, will go way beyond what is necessary or desirable.

As these examples show, forcing oneself to respect what looks like irrationality on the customer's part, forcing oneself to find the realities of the customer's situation that make it rational behaviour, may well be the most effective approach to seeing one's entire business from the point of view of market and customer. It is usually the quickest way to get outside one's own business and into market-focused action.

Marketing analysis is a good deal more than ordinary market research or customer research. It first tries to look at the entire business. And second, it tries to look not at our customer, our market, our products, but at the market, the customer, his purchases, his satisfactions, his values, his buying and spending patterns, his rationality.

7

Knowledge Is the Business

Knowledge is the business fully as much as the customer is the business. Physical goods or services are only the vehicle for the exchange of customer purchasing-power against business knowledge.

Business is a human organization, made or broken by the quality of its people. Labour might one day be done by machines to the point where it is fully automated. But knowledge is a specifically human resource. It is not found in books. Books contain information; whereas knowledge is the ability to apply information to specific work and performance. And that only comes with a human being, his brain or the skill of his hands.

For business success, knowledge must first be meaningful to the customer in terms of satisfaction and value. Knowledge *per se* is useless in business (and not only in business); it is only effective through the contribution it makes outside of the business – to customers, markets and end-uses.

To be able to do something as well as others is not enough either. It does not give the leadership position without which a business is doomed. Only excellence earns a profit; the only genuine profit is that of the innovator.

Economic results are the results of differentiation. The source of this specific differentiation, and with it of business survival and growth, is a specific, distinct knowledge possessed by a group of people in the business.

But while there is always at least one such knowledge area in every successful business, no two businesses are alike in their distinct knowledge. Here, for instance, is the specific knowledge which might seem to an outsider to characterize some well-known large businesses.

General Motors, the world's largest manufacturing company, excels in knowledge of business development, especially of businesses that produce large, highly engineered mass-produced and mass-distributed units. Having acquired this knowledge in the automobile industry, General Motors has extended it to cover diesel locomotives and heavy earth-moving equipment, as well as consumer appliances. In particular, General Motors seems to have the ability to take over a mediocre business and transform it into a successful one. There are, however, limitations; General Motors too possesses specific rather than universal knowledge. The company has not succeeded in becoming an important producer of aircraft engines. This is a different market and a different knowledge, even though the technology is close to what General Motors applies in many other areas with great success. Even within the automotive field, General Motors is not the universal management genius. Its English subsidiary Vauxhall, after forty years of General Motors ownership and management, is still a poor third in the market.

The large American commercial bank, to take another example, has to have knowledge in three areas. It has to know the management of money. It has to know the management of capital, both in its trust and its investment business. Perhaps most important is the unique knowledge of data processing which a large commercial bank has to have, since it handles figures and documents together.

IBM, as the company itself stresses, is not the leader of the office equipment industry because of its physical products, good though they are. It is the leader because it excels in the management of data and information for business needs. What it gets paid for is a service rather than a product; it earns its livelihood with its knowledge of business processes.

A large space and defence contractor – someone like the Martin Company or North American Aviation – undoubtedly has special competence in metallurgy and electronics, in aerodynamics and physics. Its really distinct knowledge, however, is systems design and systems management – in part conceptual, in part managerial – in which a great many different skills (some of them yet to be acquired) are being directed towards a job no one has ever done before. It is the ability to anticipate the unknown, to plan for the unforeseen, and to bring together productively a great many areas of ignorance that constitutes excellence in systems management.

Philips in Holland has great technical competence, to be sure. But so have two dozen or more electric-equipment makers all over. What sets Philips apart is their unique ability to build and run a truly international company. All Philips companies are fully a part of the economy, the society, the market of the country in which they operate. Yet they all have the same products; and they are all consciously and unmistakably members of a tightly knit 'family' in which everyone accepts the authority of the 'head of the house', the top management back home in Holland.

What a business is able to do with excellence may be quite humdrum, something which thousands of other businesses can do well but which this one does much better.

One division of a large and well-known company consistently earns higher profits than the rest. The division does nothing but stamp, cut, shape millions of pieces of metal – with processes and machines used in a hundred thousand metal-working shops all over the world. But this particular division does this common job with uncommon excellence. It is its boast that it can run off a sample of the final product before the potential customer has finished explaining what he is looking for; that its price rarely runs higher than half of what the customer would have been willing to pay; and that it can start delivering any metal part in commercial quantities before the customer has returned to his own office. What this division excels in is speed and simplicity of design. Indeed, it rarely has to go through the engineering-design stages. Its plant superintendents, mostly men with little formal schooling, can take a rough sketch and convert it into a production proto-type right on the machines and in practically no time.

Sometimes the knowledge that defines the business may be purely technological.

National Distillers, for instance, one of the leading manu-facturers of alcoholic beverages in the United States, defines its knowledge as fermentation chemistry. And this definition led it, shortly after World War II, into becoming a major chemical and pharmaceutical company.

But I said 'knowledge', not 'technology'. Technology – that is, the application of the physical sciences to work – is one form of knowledge. In no business is it the only necessary knowledge. There are many successful businesses in highly technological fields that do not excel in technology. They have to be technologically competent, of course. But their specific strength lies elsewhere –

for example, in marketing (as is true of at least one well-known and successful chemical company in the United States).

Thus the successful glass company that says 'our business is glass' obviously has to know more than the technology of glassmaking, complex and demanding though it is. It must have knowledge in the commercial and industrial application of glassy matter. Its knowledge is as much end-use knowledge as glassmaking knowledge.

This is always true of materials industries. Yet of all businesses they are the ones most nearly definable in terms of technology and of a distinct, organized body of information that can be taught and learned.

WHAT CAN WE DO WELL?

The best way to come to grips with one's own business knowledge is to look at the things the business has done well, and the things it apparently does poorly. This is particularly revealing if other apparently equally well-managed and competent businesses have had the opposite experience in similar undertakings. 'What have we done well – and without any sense of great strain – while somebody else has failed to do the same job?' is thus the first question. And 'What do we do poorly – while someone else seems to have no difficulty with it?' is the corollary.

Take, for instance, the contrasting performances of two exceedingly successful companies, General Electric and General Motors, in the development of new businesses. General Electric has shown outstanding ability to take a new idea and build a business on it, starting from scratch. It decided apparently during World War II that the United States could not afford to depend on imports of industrial diamonds but had to be able to make its own. From there it took only five years or so until it had found a way to make synthetic diamonds commercially. And ten years later – around 1960 – the synthetic diamond business of General Electric had become the world's largest industrial diamond supplier.

General Motors has an equally outstanding record in developing businesses. It buys them, as a rule, when they have already achieved a fairly substantial size and leadership position. Again and again it has taken a merely adequate business and, within a few years, made a champion out of it. This is so rare a talent that General Motors frequently is suspected of the twentieth-century version of witchcraft: some unfathomable anti-trust violation.

Yet neither company appears to do well what comes so easily to the other. General Motors has never, to my knowledge, started a business. And General Electric seems to have had little luck with the businesses it acquires.

Three well-known chemical companies similarly offer an illuminating contrast.

All three companies have done well over the years. To the outsider they look much alike. They all have big research centres, big plants, sales organizations, and so on. They all work in the same lines of chemistry. They are about equal in capital investment and in sales. They all show about the same substantial returns on investment. But one company always does well if it can bring a product or product line into the consumer market. The second company is outstanding in its ability to develop new chemical specialties for the industrial user. Again and again it has tried to break into the consumer market; and it has failed in the attempt again and again. The third company is not doing particularly well in either the consumer or the industrial market. Its return on sales is quite low compared to the other two. But it has tremendous income from licensing developments, coming out of its research, to other chemical companies – developments which apparently the company itself does not know how to turn into successful products and profitable sales.

The first and the third company are obviously strong in original research. The second one says of itself – and only half in jest – 'We haven't had one original idea in the last twenty years.' But it has amazing ability to see the potential of commercial development in somebody else's half-formulated idea or in a laboratory curiosity; to acquire the rights to the idea; and to convert it into saleable chemical specialties for industrial use.

Each of the three companies has come to understand what it can do and what it cannot do. Each sets its goals and measures its performance in terms of its specific knowledge: the first in terms of success in the consumer market; the second in terms of the new successful chemical specialties it develops;

the third in terms of the ratio of licence fees received to research budget.

One need not, of course, compare oneself with somebody else. One can also compare one's own failures with one's own successes, and ask: What explains our performance?

A medium-sized company, working on the instrumentation of space craft, missiles, high-speed planes, and so on, had such uneven performance that a new – and technologically rather ignorant – president was brought in to straighten it out. There seemed to be no explanation for the unevenness of the performance – there were great successes in electronics side by side with complete failures; great successes in guidance controls side by side with complete failures; great successes in optics side by side with complete failures; and so on. Nor did an analysis of the men responsible in each instance give any clue – the same men, working in the same fields, would perform quite unevenly. It was only when the projects were looked at, one by one, that the answer was found. Wherever a contract had a tight deadline, the company did well. Its specific ability was to work under pressure – then effective teams would form themselves spontaneously. Without pressure no one, it seemed, paid any attention to a contract or project. Ironically, in a well-meaning attempt to create a university atmosphere, management had worked hard to get leisurely, non-pressure contracts from the government – and had apparently succeeded only too well.

Finally, it is always a good idea to ask one's good customers, 'What do we do for you that no one else does as well?' Not that the customers always know. But their answers, however confused, are likely to bring out a pattern that indicates where to look for the answer.

KNOWLEDGE REALITIES

These examples convey five fundamentals:

1. A valid definition of the specific knowledge of a business sounds simple – deceptively so. One always excels at doing something one considers so obvious that everybody else must be able to do it too. The old saying that the erudition a man is conscious of is not learning but pedantry applies also to the specific knowledge of a business.

2. It takes practice to do a knowledge analysis well.

The first analysis may come up with embarrassing generalities such as: our business is communications, or transportation, or energy. But of course every business is communications or transportation or energy. These general terms may
make good slogans for a salesmen's convention; but to convert
them to operational meaning – that is, to do anything with them
(except to repeat them) – is impossible.

On the other extreme, one may come up with a twenty-four
volume encyclopedia of the physical sciences as a knowledge-
definition plus a complete set of handbooks on all business
functions. It is perfectly true that everyone in a managerial job
should know the fundamentals of each business function and
of every business discipline. Every manager should understand
the fundamentals of those areas of human inquiry – whether
electrical engineering, pharmacology or, in a publishing house,
the craft of the novelist – that are relevant to his business. But
no one can excel at universal knowledge – one probably cannot
even do moderately well at universal information.

But with repetition the attempt to define the knowledge of
one's own business soon becomes easy and rewarding. Few questions force a management into as objective, as searching, as productive a look at itself as the question: What is our specific
knowledge?

3. Few answers moreover are as important as the answer to
this question. Knowledge is a perishable commodity. It has to be
reaffirmed, relearned, repractised all the time. One has to work
constantly at regaining one's specific excellence. But how can one
work at maintaining one's excellence unless one knows what it is?

4. Every knowledge eventually becomes the wrong knowledge.
It becomes obsolete. The question should always arise: What *else*
do we need? Or do we need something different?

'Have our recent experiences borne out our previous conclusions that this particular ability gives us leadership?' the
president of a successful Japanese chemical company asks each
of his top men once every six months. He himself analyses the
performance of each product, in each market and with each
important customer, to see whether actual experience is in line
with the expectations and predictions of his knowledge analysis.
He asks each of his top men – from research director to controller and personnel man – to do the same analysis. And he

spends one of his quarterly three-day management meetings on knowledge analysis. He credits his growth – within a decade this formerly limited and fairly small company has become one of the world's leading producers in a major field – to reviewing knowledge effectiveness and knowledge needs.

5. Finally, no company can excel in many knowledge areas.

Most companies – like the most people – find it hard enough to be merely competent in a single area. This, of course, means that most businesses remain marginal and just manage to hang on. The figures amply confirm this. Out of each hundred businesses started, seventy-five or so die before their fifth birthday with management failure as the leading cause of death.

A business may be able to excel in more than one area. A successful business has to be at least competent in a good many knowledge areas in addition to being excellent in one. And many businesses have to achieve beyond the ordinary in more than one area. But to have real knowledge of the kind for which the market offers economic rewards requires concentration on doing a few things superbly well.

HOW GOOD IS OUR KNOWLEDGE?

The knowledge analysis, like the market analysis, leads to diagnostic questions.

1. Do we have the right knowledge? Do we concentrate where the results are? For the answer one looks to the marketing analysis of the business. The right knowledge is the knowledge needed to exploit the market opportunities. Does the business have the knowledge needed to give it leadership position in the market, and to earn rewards where the market values excellence?

It is an unusual business that finds that its knowledge is entirely wrong for the market. Such a business is likely to have died long before it got around to analysing itself. But it is highly probable – in any business – that the existing specific knowledge is inadequate to the need.

There is often need for learning new things. Papermakers, for instance, had to become polymer chemists of considerable skill. And when the computer came in, the old punch-card salesmen of IBM had to move into an entirely new world and learn an entirely different language.

Sometimes the balance of knowledges has to be shifted. What was the core knowledge of the business has to be subordinated.

Thus, in the steel industry, during the last twenty years, the dominant knowledge has shifted from making steel to marketing steel. With the advent of modern metallurgy, making steel has increasingly become a matter of building performance into the equipment rather than practising a mysterious alchemy. It is not becoming less important, but it is becoming increasingly less possible to excel in production. Steel marketing, however, what with the tremendous variations in the economic and technical characteristics and results of different product mixes, is infinitely more crucial than it used to be when the main job was to sell tonnage.

Knowledge has to progress to remain knowledge.

Knowledge is indeed very much like a world record in athletics. For years it stands, apparently immovable. Then one sprinter runs the mile a little faster, one pole-vaulter jumps a little higher – and suddenly other athletes repeat the feat and have acquired a new dimension of performance. For what one man has done, another one can always do again; and this is particularly true with respect to excellence.

2. The analysis of knowledge leads to a set of questions as to how effectively the right knowledge is being used.

Are we actually getting paid for the knowledge we contribute?

This does not necessarily mean that one has to bill the customer for the knowledge. IBM bills for equipment. But both IBM and the customer know that knowledge is the essential thing, and that the customer buys service rather than product. Indeed, it is this awareness on both sides that explains why IBM, starting late and with reluctance, took the leadership in the computer field away from companies that had started earlier and that seemed to possess much greater technical competence.

3. Is our knowledge sufficiently built into our goods and services?

One example is a company that has basic knowledge in polymer chemistry – perhaps its greatest knowledge area. Yet 90 per cent of its products do not benefit from this knowledge at all, even though they are polymer chemicals. They are still made by the old 'cook-book' method of trial and error without application of the scientific and technical knowledge which the company has and which the customer expects when he buys its products.

4. How can we improve? What are we missing? And how do we go about supplying it?

Most commercial banks, for instance, have not yet realized that their data-processing knowledge might lead to a profitable business. It might enable them to offer office management service to middle-sized business, business that is too small to have its own modern equipment, and too large not to use modern methods of record keeping and data processing.

Or, to give another example, the large defence and space contractor – especially with the expected levelling-off of U.S. government spending in these areas – might apply his systems management knowledge to such new fields as the exploration of the ocean, or the redesign of our oldest (but totally undesigned) system, the large hospital.

The conclusions of the knowledge analysis must be fed back into the marketing analysis to bring out market opportunities that might have been missed or underrated. And the conclusions of the market analysis are projected on the knowledge analysis to bring out needs for new or changed knowledge.

8

This Is Our Business

The analyses sketched out in the preceding chapters should provide the executive with an understanding of the business adequate to the demands of his economic task. No one of the four will do the job singlehanded. But by putting together:

The analysis of results, revenues, resources;

The analysis of cost centres and cost structure;

The marketing analysis;

The knowledge analysis;

a business should be able to understand itself; to diagnose itself; and to direct itself.

There remains one essential step: to re-examine the *tentative diagnosis* in the light of the marketing and knowledge analyses. As a result – and this can be said dogmatically – it will have to be changed substantially. Even though the 'facts' were recorded precisely at the tentative stage, they could not yet be truly understood.

Some of the products will require a change of classification, for example. An unjustified specialty may turn out to be a highly promising product – for a different market or in a different distributive channel. Conversely, what looked in the tentative diagnosis like a strong product, a today's breadwinner still in its prime, or maybe even a tomorrow's breadwinner, may turn out to be at or near the end of its life-span.

Some products will be found to need substantial modification. The same holds for markets, for distributive channels, and sometimes for whole businesses.

A major aluminium company had about decided that the market for aluminium foil was saturated, and that therefore poorly selling foil products were doing as well as could be expected. But the company ran the foil business like other aluminium lines; that is, as a producer-goods business, selling to design engineers and industrial purchasing agents. A marketing analysis forced management reluctantly to accept that this was a consumer-goods business in which the retailer – especially the supermarket – was the real customer. The company separated the foil business managerially from its other businesses and entrusted it to people who had never been inside an aluminium mill but knew how to market consumer goods. The foil business, a few years later, had not only reached but exceeded the original expectations; though a comparative newcomer in aluminium foil, the company is now close to first rank in its national market.

The experience of a rather small and highly specialized chemical company illustrates reclassification of both markets and knowledge and the resulting change in the diagnosis of a product – and in the strategy of a business. For many years the family-owned and family-managed company had produced a line of intermediates for the manufacture of textile dyes, especially dyestuffs for cotton. Main customers were the big chemical companies which do not make all the intermediates for a full dyestuff line themselves. But as synthetic fibres took over more and more of the American textile industry, this company saw its market and its profits shrinking steadily. Market analysis led the management to ask: 'Where is *the* market?' whereas formerly the question had always been, 'Where is *our* market?' This brought out that the market for cotton textiles, and with it for cotton dyes, was far from shrinking. It was actually expanding faster than the synthetic market. Only it was expanding not in the industrially developed countries, but in Latin America, India, Pakistan, Africa, Hong Kong, and so on. In each of these countries dyes had to be imported. There was nothing wrong with the company's products; they were just in the wrong market.

The company has now gone international. It makes dyestuff intermediates in eleven industrially developing countries, ranging from Israel to Formosa, and from Nigeria to India. In every case the capital risk has been taken by somebody in the host country. The American manufacturer supplies the technical knowledge and the management under a long-term management contract, and against a fee and a stock participation.

At home the same company also changed the business as a result of its knowledge analysis. While still making its old dyestuff intermediates, it is rapidly expanding as a designer and manufacturer of chemical engineering equipment for dyestuff manufacture. This puts to good use specific and distinct knowledge in the design and manufacturing of dyestuff-making equipment. But until the executives analysed the company's knowledge, they did not even realize that they had this capacity, let alone that it was an asset in today's rapidly industrializing world.

Another example illustrates the consequences of redefining the customer.

The redesign of the entire line of a hospital equipment maker resulted from a study of the market. The company had always assumed that acceptance by the medical profession meant leadership and success for its products. It spend a good deal of time and money on promoting itself and its products with the doctors. And it designed its products around their concepts of value, utility and excellence. It had the esteem of the doctors – but it did not do well in selling to hospitals.

Analysis showed that doctors do not buy hospital equipment. It is bought by administrators who, whether they have the M.D. degree or not, have to run a complex institution – and run it primarily with poorly paid and not particularly skilled personnel. Their concept of 'excellence' is equipment that neither ties down scarce, highly skilled nurses and technicians nor requires a lot of training – equipment which relatively unskilled people can operate safely, without danger to the patient, to themselves, or to the equipment. As the company described it: 'We found out that our equipment has to be end-use focused and therefore has to be "moron-proof" rather than "doctor focused" and sophisticated.'

This, by the way, also led to a radical reclassification of costs and to a change in the deployment of scarce resources. Promotion with the medical profession had been a major cost point for this company – and the ablest people on the sales staff worked at it personally. It had been considered the most productive cost in the entire cost stream. The cost of presenting the equipment to the hospital professions, however, was considered near-waste. The promotional effort with the doctors, while not abandoned, has now been cut down – it is more or less considered support, or at best a means to prevent opposition rather than to create the market. But promotional efforts to hospital administrators and hospital employees – including, incidentally, close co-operation with the training directors of hospital employee unions – is now seen as a truly productive cost which deserves high attention.

Here are two examples from a service industry:

A major life insurance company had developed a policy especially designed for the middle-class family man in his thirties or forties, the junior executive, the younger but already established professional man, and so on. The special attraction of the policy, the company thought, was that it enabled the insured to tailor the policy to his family situation and needs and yet retain a rather low premium-base. The policy sold no better than any other policy. Analysis of the way the customer buys showed what was wrong with it; it was being sold in the evening because this was the only time the 'prospect' was likely to be at home. Yet he did not want to spend a lot of time discussing an insurance policy in the evenings. After a day's hard work he wanted to be left alone. The salesman therefore rarely got a chance even to explain the policy. But the analysis also showed that the wife in these families is vitally interested in financial protection and knows at least as much as the husband about the family situation. And she has time during the day. Hence the policy is now being sold – with good results – to the wives in the morning hours and after an appointment has been set up by telephone or letter. They then 'sell' the policy to their husbands.

Another company thought that it was doing quite well with a complete insurance package – automobile, fire, home and household, health and accident, life insurance, all in one master contract sold by one salesman in one call. But customer analysis showed that casualty insurance and life insurance are different aggregates in the customer's mind. They should be; they serve entirely different needs. (That both are insurance is of no conceivable importance to the customer, however relevant it may seem to the companies, to the actuaries, and to the state governments and their insurance commissioners.) Separating the two – having one casualty package and one life insurance package – helped greatly. It also brought out that a good many prospective buyers would have bought one or the other but bought neither when offered both in one package. What helped even more was adding a non-insurance to the life package, mutual investment-trust shares. For life insurance is finance to the customer; and an equity investment not only fits in with it, but makes a complete investment programme out of a life insurance policy. This has been so successful that within a few years half a dozen big insurers (for instance the Sears-Roebuck-owned All-State Insurance Company) have started imitating the new finance package.

These are, of course, examples of actions taken, rather than just of reclassification or redefinition. But every action emerged from re-examining a tentative diagnosis in the light of market and knowledge analyses.

WHAT IS LACKING?

Even more important than to reinterpret what the business is doing is to identify what the business should be doing but so far does not do. Market and knowledge analyses, when projected upon the earlier analyses of the business, will bring out what is lacking.

In the result areas, three gaps are so often encountered that they can almost be expected. The business may need a major *development* effort to replace what is clearly past its prime. The replacement needed may be a product. But it may also be a new area of business effort and activity, such as a new market, new end-uses, or different distributive channels. And while not 'technical' in the usual sense of the term, developing a new market or a new distribution system is as much 'design and development' – and requires as much knowledge, work and money – as designing a new piece of equipment.

The second common gap is lack of *adequate support* to exploit opportunity and success.

Market analysis in an equipment making company revealed, for instance, that a major product, while highly praised in one industrial market, was not bought by it to any extent. A competitor's product, though considered both more expensive and less satisfactory, got the orders. The competitor offered a complete package consisting of the piece of machinery in question plus a power-drive which geared it into the rest of the customer's equipment. The irony was that the lagging company had such a power-drive, had indeed originally designed the machinery around it. Somehow – no one could ever figure out how – the sales department had become convinced that the drive did not suit the particular industry to which the machine was being sold.

There are similar oversights in every business. No management is blessed with omniscience; unless one's vision is systematically sharpened, one overlooks the most obvious things or misinterprets the clearest signs.

The gap may lie in the distributive channel: the business has the products and services. It promotes the goods. It may even persuade the potential customers. But when they want to buy, the product is not available where they shop. The distributive channel does not reach them, or it is clogged halfway.

Every change in a product or in the way it is presented requires a thorough review of distributive channels. And every change in distributive structure, in turn – for instance, the rush to mass retail distribution in the American economy since World War II – requires a review of product design and product line, customers, markets and end-uses in turn.

The outside analyses usually reveal a third gap in *knowledge needs* and *opportunities*. What new knowledge of real importance is needed? Where does existing core knowledge need improvement, updating and advancement? Where does our knowledge need redefinition?

The first two needs are straightforward enough. It is the last that is generally overlooked – and yet it is often the most important. Here is an example:

Knowledge of the printing industry, ability to service a printer, understanding of a printer's business, may be the marketing knowledge of a fine-paper company. But it may need redefinition as reproduction-market knowledge or as graphic arts-market knowledge to enable the company to market to the new reproduction-paper customers, who are the owners of office-reproduction equipment. This will require learning a few new things – for businesses to whom paper is an incidental supply buy quite differently from commercial printers for whom paper is the basic and most expensive raw material. But the important new factor may well be simply a clear redefinition. Otherwise, the paper people will not use what is applicable of their old knowledge in the new market. They may even throw away their present leadership position.

Having reached the end of this self-analysis, the businessman should be able to see what the business is, what it does, and what it can do. He should be able to determine:

The satisfactions his products or services aim to provide, the wants they should fill, and the contribution for which the business can expect to get paid.

The knowledge areas in which the business has to have excellence to make the desired contribution. It should be possible to define what the business has to do better than anybody else to earn the chance to survive and to prosper. This carries with it a decision on the human values and the human resources needed.

The customers, markets, and end-uses to whom the business contributes distinctive value; and the distributive channels that have to be developed – and satisfied as customers – to reach these customers, markets and end-uses.

The technology, processes, product or services areas in which these objectives find implementation and through which they take physical, tangible form.

The leadership position required in each result area.

Marketing analysis and knowledge-analysis, when superimposed on the analysis of results, revenues, resources and on the analysis of cost structure and cost centres, should not only yield new facts. They should give a management the knowledge to say: 'This is our business'; the vision to say: 'This is what our business could be'; and the sense of direction needed to say: 'And this is how we might get from where we are to where we could be.'

PART II

FOCUS ON
OPPORTUNITY

9

Building on Strength

Analysis of the entire business and its basic economics always shows it to be in worse disrepair than anyone expected. The products everyone boasts of turn out to be yesterday's bread-winners or investments in managerial ego. Activities to which no one paid much attention turn out to be major cost centres and so expensive as to endanger the competitive position of the company. What everyone in the business believes to be quality turns out to have little meaning to the customer. Important and valuable knowledge either is not applied where it could produce results or produces results no one uses. I know more than one executive who fervently wished at the end of the analysis that he could forget all he had learned and go back to the old days of the 'rat race' when 'sufficient unto the day was the crisis thereof'.

But precisely because there are so many different areas of importance, the day-by-day method of management is inadequate even in the smallest and simplest business. Because deterioration is what happens normally – that is, unless somebody counteracts it – there is need for a systematic and purposeful programme. There is need to reduce the almost limitless possible tasks to a manageable number. There is need to concentrate scarce resources on the greatest opportunities and results. There is need to do the few right things and do them with excellence.

To make business effective the executive has available three well-tried and tested approaches:

1. He can start with a model of the 'ideal business' which would produce maximum results from the available markets and knowledge – or at least those results that, over a long period, are likely to be most favourable.

2. He can try to maximize opportunities by focusing the available resources on the most attractive possibilities and devoting them to obtaining the greatest possible results.

3. He can maximize resources so that those opportunities are found – if not created – that endow the available high-quality resources with the greatest possible impact.

The rise of every one of the truly great enterprises in economic history was based on these approaches.

The Rise of General Motors

An example of the ideal business approach is the rise of General Motors, both the world's largest automobile company and the world's largest manufacturing enterprise. Alfred P. Sloan, Jr, who first redesigned General Motors and then, as chief executive for almost thirty years, built the company, has told the story in a recent book.* General Motors was on the verge of collapse when he took over in the depression of 1921. Ford with one model had a 60 per cent share of the American automobile market. General Motors with eight models was a weak second with about 12 per cent of the market. Only two of the eight models were profitable, six were losers – and had been losing not only money but market standing as well.

Sloan began by thinking through what the ideal automobile company in the American market would look like. He came out with a design in which five models covered the market. Only two of the existing models – the Buick and the Cadillac, both at the upper end of the line – fitted into this design. Three models were completely abandoned. Three others were replaced by what amounted to a brand new car even though it retained the old name. Sloan actually practised the total marketing approach thirty years before the term was coined.

The Sloan design changed the concept of car marketing and the approach to the customer. Each of his five models was placed in a price and performance class in which it was both the most expensive and best-performing car of a lower price range and the cheapest and simplest car of the next-higher one. For a fairly small additional sum the low-income customer could obtain a car which, in appearance as well as in performance, was well above the Ford Model T. The customer who could afford a medium-priced car could also save a little money by buying the low-priced car with most of the appearance and performance of the medium-priced line; or he could pay a little more and have a near-luxury car. Each of the five cars was a distinct entry into the market and designed to be the leader in its class. Yet each competed also with

* *My Years with General Motors* (New York: Doubleday, 1964).

the GM car on either side of it. For Sloan rightly believed that unchallenged success was dangerous, and so provided each of his five makes with at least one strong challenger from within the family.

This design made General Motors within five years both the dominant American automobile manufacturer and by far the most profitable one. And when Ford itself hit the comeback trail after World War II, it deliberately adopted the Sloan design and imported executives from General Motors who had been reared in the Sloan concept and strategy.

For the early 1920s, Sloan's design was radical – so radical indeed that it was quite a few years before his associates at General Motors accepted it. It violated all the then 'known facts'. Instead of dividing the potential customers sharply into a mass-market wanting uniform automobiles at the lowest possible price, and a class-market with low volume and high prices, Sloan saw the customers as essentially homogeneous, demanding mass-production but also performance, low price and easy sale of a used car but also an annual model change, comfort and styling.

Sloan did not try to dislodge Ford by doing just as well, nor even by doing better. He never considered doing again what Ford had done before; that is, building the cheapest, standardized, changeless car. Instead, he made the Model T obsolete through something which neither Ford (nor anyone else) could possibly produce: the one-year-old, secondhand car. It had been the new car only one year earlier. As 'transportation' it could easily compete with the Model T. It had the appearance, styling and performance of the high-priced cars, but was cheaper even than the Model T.

Till then the used-car market had been considered a nuisance by the car makers. Sloan saw that it was the real volume market; and that the manufacturer had to design, sell and service his new car both for greatest sale this year and for easiest resale a year or two hence.

In the medium-priced car market, Sloan found price differentiation to be less important. But here the role of the car as prestige symbol was greatest. This meant deliberately creating customer identification with specific makes, expressed through distinctive styling with fair continuity. Buick, for instance, was to identify itself with the successful professional man, through its styling, its pricing, its selling and its promotion.

For the top-price range Sloan's question was: What is the

highest-priced car that still can be sold in such volume as to justify mass-production? In its way this too was an original and heretical approach. It had been axiomatic that the luxury car had to be hand-made and hand-crafted with production small and price high. General Motors' Cadillac, before Sloan, had followed this policy with considerable success. Yet Sloan replaced the profitable hand-crafted Cadillac with a volume-produced, assembly-made car, which while costing less than a hand-made car, actually exceeded in performance all but the Rolls-Royce. Just as Chevrolet became, within a few years, the standard of the low-priced range, so Cadillac became the standard of the high-priced range.

It should be emphasized that Sloan's design was neither flash of genius nor product of years of hard toil with mathematical models and complicated computer runs. Sloan had, of course, given a good deal of thought to the automobile market before he took on General Motors. But his direct concern till then had mainly been the accessory business rather than the automobile business. He did not have a big staff for his study. He worked with a small committee of company executives and had only one month for the job. He did the work primarily from observation of the market and by asking questions of his own executives and of automobile dealers.

In other words: the results of a fairly short and simple study, while crude, are good enough to serve as the foundation for major decisions and actions. The work can be done by ordinary techniques available to managers (though more sophisticated techniques should, of course, be used wherever they speed the work).

Alfred P. Sloan's grand design took a good many years to execute. Pontiac for instance really did not become the car Sloan had specified until almost fifteen years later. But from the beginning the design produced results. And this has been the experience wherever the ideal business approach, the approach that designs a business to be what the market wants, has been tried.

THE FIRST INNOVATORS

The second major approach asks: What are the opportunities for the greatest economic results?

The best illustrations of the maximization of opportunity are the two men who, independently of each other, created the electrical industry and indeed our electrified world of today: the German,

Werner von Siemens (1816–92) and the American, Thomas A. Edison (1847–1931). Together their impact on the world we live in has been a good deal greater than that of Henry Ford and Alfred P. Sloan.

One answer to the question: 'What did Siemens invent?' is: the first practical electric generator. But one can also answer: the electric apparatus industry. To the question: 'What did Edison invent?' one can answer: the electric light bulb. But one can also answer: the electric power and light industry. More than anyone else they developed methods of technological research. But there were many other men at the time working on the same inventions. One can even argue that every one of their inventions was either anticipated or perfected at the same time by someone else.* Yet only these two men designed and built major new industries.

They knew very well what they were doing. They were by no means alone in being excited by the new vistas opened up by the scientific developments in electricity, especially by the work of the great Faraday. But they alone asked: What are the major economic opportunities which this knowledge opens up? What in the way of new or additional technological invention and development is needed to realize this economic opportunity? Siemens did not develop the electric railway because he had a generator; he developed the generator because he had visualized the electric railway as a major industry, especially for travel within the city, and therefore needed an electric motor to provide traction. Similarly Edison did not design the first light and power plant, complete with generating stations, transformers and distribution system, because he had invented a practical light bulb. He went to work on the light bulb because it was the one thing missing in his design of an integrated city-wide power and light industry.†

These men, in other words, were the first real 'innovators'. They systematically defined the opportunity for new knowledge and new capacity to achieve – that is, the opportunity for innovation. Then they set to work to provide the needed new knowledge, capacity and technology. They were also, it should be said, the first genuine 'systems designers'.

* As does, for instance, the Fifth Volume (1850–1900) of the well-known *History of Technology* (edited by Charles Singer, Oxford University Press, 1958) with its unconcealed British bias.

† Edison's latest biography, *Edison*, by Matthew Josephson (New York: McGraw Hill Book Co., 1959) brings this out fully.

Both lived a long productive life; but both were major figures by the time they were thirty; both had by that time already created new industries rather than merely a new piece of equipment or a new design. Both maximized economic opportunities by asking the question: In what area of application of electricity does the opportunity lie for the most successful and most profitable new industry?

Maximizing opportunity does not necessarily mean technological innovation, as shown by the development of Japan as a modern industrial nation.

In the period between 1870 and 1900 when Japan turned herself from a pre-industrial economy of rural clans into the first non-Western modern economy, Japan could not possibly have promoted technological innovation. Her problem was rather that of social innovation: to create the institutions which would enable a thoroughly non-Western country with its own culture, tradition and social structure to accept and use Western technology and economics.

The great family businesses – the Zaibatsu – who carried forward Japan's economic development in this period, consistently maximized opportunities. They asked: Which industries, at the present stage of our development, offer the greatest economic opportunities to Japan and to our business? The answer might be: a steamship line; a life insurance company; a textile industry; and so on. This, in turn, led to the identification of needs for social innovation – for instance, the need for a factory organization that would merge Japanese traditions of personal and social relationships with the discipline of modern industrial production. It is because of the conscious focus on maximizing opportunities that Japan succeeded in doing what no other non-Western country has done so far: to develop a modern economy fairly fast and with a minimum of social dislocation and political upheaval.

Successful planning is always based on maximizing opportunities. Soviet planning rests on a theory that sees in the entrepreneur the agent who maximizes opportunities for capital investment. (See Chapter 11 for a short description of the origin of this concept; its first practical application by the Brothers Pereire in their banking venture, the *Credit Mobilier*; and its impact throughout Europe.)

But there are many smaller and no less successful examples. Sears Roebuck in the United States and Marks & Spencer in Great

Britain, two leading retail businesses of today, have consistently asked themselves: Which are the opportunties where doing something new and different is likely to have the greatest economic results? Their experience shows that this is a dynamic question, which produces new answers every few years – whereas an ideal business, once designed and effective, is likely to retain its characteristics for a fairly long period.

How the Rothschilds Grew

For the third approach, that of maximizing resources, there is no more instructive example than the rise of the House of Rothschild. It was anything but a foregone conclusion. In the late 1790s Meyer Amschel Rothschild, the founder of the dynasty, was still only a small-town moneylender, barely known in the main centres of international finance. Less than twenty years later, at the end of the Napoleonic Wars, the House of Rothschild was the unchallenged financial great power of Europe, treating with other great powers such as France or Russia as an equal, and barely polite to minor princes and potentates. What had catapulted the Rothschilds to success in that short period was systematic maximization of the resources of the family.

The family had four first-rate resources in the four older sons, Nathan, James, Amschel and Salomon. For each their father (or more probably their mother) found and selected the major opportunity best fitted for his talent and character, the opportunity where the individual 'resource' could make its greatest contribution.

Nathan was the ablest, daring and highly imaginative. But he was uncouth and arrogant. He was given London – at the time the greatest financial centre in the world, but also a ruthlessly competitive market where financial and economic power was daily being fought for by aggressive business professionals who cared nothing for manners and counted only hard cash.

Napoleon's Paris went to James. Paris was then – and for a century to come – the greatest capital market on the continent. It was also the most treacherous spot in the financial universe. The financial conspiracies and plots in the novels of Balzac – James Rothschild's contemporary – were only partly fiction. Spies, paid by government or by competitors, were everywhere. Finance was a political business; yet political upheaval – revolution, terror, tyranny and restoration – were endemic and destroyed many mightier financial powers than the Rothschilds then were or could expect to be for years to come. But this was just the spot for James – in fact he might have been misplaced anywhere else. He throve on intrigue and had been the political strategist of the family from early years.

Salomon, courteous, patient and dignified to the point of pomposity, went to Vienna where banking still meant dealing with one client, the Hapsburg Court, with its interminable delay and indecision, its stiff ceremonial and its self-important aristocracy. Frankfurt finally, though home to the Rothschilds, was the least important of all financial centres in Europe. It became the seat of the family's 'general manager', the industrious, conscientious Amschel who loved nothing better than the back office. He kept his brothers informed through voluminous handwritten letters. He built and ran the far-flung private network of information and intelligence which – before the age of daily newspaper, post office, telegraph and telephone – gave the Rothschilds a near-monopoly on fast and dependable knowledge of world affairs. His greatest contribution was probably in the personnel field. He found, recruited and largely trained the German-Jewish boys with a passion for anonymity who as confidential clerks and managers became the backbone of the business.

What the Rothschilds did not do is, however, even more revealing. They did not assign to Kalmann, the fifth son, any opportunity whatever. Instead they sent him to Naples – one royal court where there was no business, and where therefore no major damage could be done to the Rothschild standing or to their fortunes. There would have been plenty of important opportunities had the family wanted Kalmann to have one. Both Hamburg and Amsterdam were important enough to warrant establishing business partners and agencies there. The Rothschilds also were aware of the opportunities of the fledgling United States across the Atlantic. But Kalmann had neither superior ability nor superior industry, at least not by Rothschild standards. And it is the one absolute rule in maximizing resources that one never entrusts an opportunity to a non-resource, that is to mediocrity. It cannot turn the opportunity into advantage. But to every opportunity corresponds a risk; mediocrity is therefore bound to harm if entrusted with opportunity. If one has a fifth son and, as a family, has to take care of him adequately, it is cheaper to support him in royal style out of harm's way than to put him in charge of opportunities.

What is important is not that General Motors, Edison, and the Rothschilds became great and strong; it is that they started near the bottom. Whether the penniless Prussian officer Seimens, or the half-deaf, almost unschooled, errand boy Edison; the provincial, awkward – not to mention Jewish – Rothschilds in a world of prejudiced, arrogant aristocrats, or the undeveloped Japanese clans of 1860; they all started with nothing, except a systematic approach. Even General Motors, while a large corporation for the America of 1920, was a poor second to Ford. One can argue, of course, that even without any such approach Siemens and Edison would have been notable inventors, the Rothschilds well-known bankers, and General Motors a sizeable company. What gave them leadership, however, was the systematic approach with which they applied their ability to the opportunities time and history had put within their grasp.

All three approaches have one thing in common: they build on strength; they look for opportunities rather than for problems; they stress attainable results rather than dangers to be avoided. In fact they are complementary. Each serves a distinct function and purpose. Together they convert the insight of analysis into a *programme for effective action.*

Thinking through the design of the ideal business determines the direction a company should take to attain effectiveness. It sets fundamental objectives. It establishes the theoretical optimum of economic performance against which actual results can be measured.

Maximizing opportunities shows how to move the business from yesterday to today – thereby making it ready for the new challenges of tomorrow. It shows the existing activities that should be pushed and those that should be abandoned. And it brings out the new things that might multiply results in the market or in the company's field of knowledge.

Maximizing resources, finally, is the step from insight to action. It establishes priorities. And by concentrating resources on priorities it ensures that energy and efforts go to work where performance can produce the greatest results.

TARGETS AND TIME

The design of the ideal business sets the direction. It also makes it possible to set targets – for efforts as well as for results.

The ideal-business design controls itself through feed-back from its results to its own validity. The closer a business approaches the design, the greater should its profitability be. When profitability ceases to go up even though the actual business is still approaching the ideal, the design needs restudy. In all probability it has become obsolete. After all, even the best design does not last forever. Mr Sloan's proved valid for an unusually long time – thirty-five years, until the Edsel failure of 1957. For Ford in its comeback after World War II had imitated the Sloan design; and the Edsel was to be the last, major element in a Ford Motor Company reconstructed on the lines of Sloan's earlier General Motors masterpiece.

One important element in the ideal-business design is establishment of the time period which is the proper 'present' for any given business; it varies greatly.

The best illustrations are the contrasting fortunes of two companies in the aircraft industry. Curtiss Wright and the Martin Company. Curtiss Wright, in the late 'forties, was the stronger company: the second-largest aircraft-engine builder in the United States, solidly established as a leader in both civilian and military engines, with a heavy backlog of orders and great financial resources. Martin by contrast was an ailing air-frame builder without a product of distinction, deeply in debt, and altogether, it seemed, an ageing 'war baby' without a future. But a new management at Martin came up with a present of eight to ten years as the time needed to develop a new technology in large-scale systems work. Research of shorter duration made not much sense and could not pay off. This also meant that the business had to be something that did not exist in 1950: a space business rather than an improved aircraft business.

Curtiss Wright without an analysis of this kind stayed with the time period of World War II, when the emphasis was on production rather than on new design. Its present was one to two years. Although it spent perhaps more money than any other aircraft company on research and development, Curtiss

Wright had all but disappeared as a business a decade later. Its definition of the present made management reject any project that did not promise a pay-off within twenty-four months. As a result not one of its many research projects produced anything. The Martin Company, by contrast, established a leading and successful space systems business with a relatively modest research outlay.

There is equally a present for the market, that is a period within which market results are significant.

General Motors had learned by the mid-'twenties that the time-span of the present in the automobile market was five years – a complete cycle including one very good year, one poor one, and three fair ones. The logic of the second-hand car market dictated this. General Motors built this cycle into capital investments, appraisals of performance, and the planning of development work. Capital investment, according to an oft-published formula,* was judged by the expected return over the five-year cycle at an average capacity utilization of 80 per cent. If the expected return over the cycle fell below a certain figure, or if expected capacity utilization ran below 80 per cent on average, the investment proposal was not considered acceptable. Similarly, the minimum span of technical development work was set – apparently not much later – at the three years needed to make any but minor style changes in automotive design, and the maximum (except for basic research work) at the five years that were the present of the automobile market.

As these examples show, determining the time-span that is the present of a company or industry largely determines what kind of efforts will be made. Efforts that promise results in less time are likely to be a waste not only of time, but of resources and money. To set too short a time-span and ban all efforts exceeding this period (as Curtiss Wright did) is to condemn a company to sterility.

Perhaps the best way to go about designing the ideal business is to start with a broad sketch and to correct and refine as one goes along. Otherwise one may still be rewriting, polishing and refining when the design has already become obsolete. The important thing is to get major results fast. For the largest part of the improvement

* Apparently first published as early as 1927.

in performance and results should come as soon as the business has begun to move with determination towards its vision. The first steps should be big ones.

FROM YESTERDAY TO TODAY

Maximizing opportunities looks for those seven-league steps towards realizing the ideal business and obtaining rapidly the greatest benefits possible.

By projecting the ideal business design on the analysis of the existing business all the products, markets, distribution channels, cost centres, activities and efforts of the business can be sorted out into *three categories:*

> One high-priority group where the real push has to be made, because there is a great opportunity to achieve extraordinary results.
>
> One high-priority group where the opportunity lies in not-doing; that is, in rapid and purposeful abandonment.
>
> One large and heterogeneous group of also-rans – products, markets, knowledge work, and so on – in which neither efforts to excel nor abandonment promise significant results.

To call abandonment an 'opportunity' may come as a surprise. Yet, planned, purposeful abandonment of the old and of the unrewarding is a prerequisite to successful pursuit of the new and highly promising. Above all, abandonment is the key to innovation – both because it frees the necessary resources and because it stimulates the search for the new that will replace the old.

Push areas and abandonment complement each other and therefore deserve equal priority.

The *push priorities* are easily identified. What should be pushed are those areas where the results, if successful, produce their costs many times over. These are invariably the products or markets that fit most closely the ideal-business design.

> The General Motors' experience is characteristic. Buick and Cadillac, the two makes that were profitable in 1921 and had market leadership, were also the only two of the company's eight makes which fitted the ideal-business design.

Typical result areas which deserve priority are, for instance:

> Tomorrow's breadwinners and sleepers.

The development efforts needed to replace tomorrow's breadwinner the day after tomorrow.

Important new knowledge and new distributive channels.

Cutting back high support costs, high policing costs and waste in the cost structure.

The areas of high potential are rarely over-supplied with resources. Hence what matters is not whether the budget for such an area is too high but whether it is high enough for results.

The *candidates for abandonment* are also usually fairly obvious.

There is first the investment in managerial ego. Unjustified specialties are also on the list. Then there are unnecessary support activities, and waste that can be eliminated without major effort.

Yesterday's breadwinner should almost always be abandoned on a fairly fast schedule. It still may produce net revenue. But it soon becomes a bar to the introduction and success of tomorrow's breadwinner. One should, therefore, abandon yesterday's breadwinner *before* one really wants to, let alone before one has to.

Altogether, whenever the cost of incremental acquisition is more than one-half of the likely return, there is a candidate for abandonment. It is not good enough that an activity does not appear to cost any money. It should produce results to be kept on. And the hidden costs of any activity are always much greater than anybody assumes or than any accounting system shows.

To keep a man on the payroll always costs at least three times his wage or salary. He needs space to work in, heat, light and a locker in the washroom. He needs materials to work with, supplies, a telephone, and so on. He needs a supervisor. In a hundred hidden ways he creates costs.

Every proposal for abandonment is opposed. The arguments that can be advanced to justify retention of the resultless, unpromising and unrewarding are rarely more than excuses. Most common is the plea:

We must grow; we cannot afford to shrink.

But growth, after all, is the result of success, of offering what the market wants, buys and pays for, of using economic resources effectively, and of making the profits needed for expansion and for the risks of the future. General Motors either abandoned or

mpletely made over six of the eight makes in the line – and the
sult was tremendous growth.

The argument is also sophistry. It confuses fat with muscle, and
usy-ness with economic accomplishment. Activities which do not
produce results waste substance. They are a burden – the way
overweight is a burden on the strength of a human being.

A management in an expanding economy needs to be growth-
conscious. But growth means exploiting the opportunities that the
economy offers. It does not mean doing the wrong things to get
volume. The volume will come soon enough if a business concentrates on doing the right things.

There are in each business products, services, activities and
efforts which are neither clear candidates for concentrated major
work nor candidates for abandonment: the large number of *also-
rans* which form the third category to be considered.

Among them will be today's breadwinners and frequently
the productive specialties. Here also will be cost centres which,
while representing a sizeable cost burden, can be reduced only
by efforts out of proportion to the probable results. And here
will be found the repair jobs of all kinds and descriptions, the
products, services, markets, and so on, which might become
worth while if only some major change or modification were
made.

The main rule for also-rans is that they must not absorb resources at the expense of the high opportunity areas. Only if
resources are left over after the high opportunity areas have
received all the support they need, should the also-rans be considered. And high-grade resources already committed to also-rans
should be kept there only if they cannot make a bigger contribution
in a high opportunity task.

In practice, additional resources can rarely be spared for also-
rans. And only the productive specialty among them normally
deserves all the resources it employs. The others will almost always
be found to absorb resources that would be more productive elsewhere.

Also-rans therefore have to make do with what they have – or
with less. They are put on 'milking status': as long as they yield
results, they will be kept – and milked. They will, however, not be
'fed'. And as soon as these 'milk cows' go into rapid decline, they
should be slaughtered.

THE FORWARD PROJECTION

Upgrading the existing business leads to doing things better. But what are the different things that ought to be done?

Here there are two distinct categories of opportunities:

Replacements of present products, activities and efforts which are almost right, by products, activities and efforts that are completely right.

Innovations, the highest-opportunity group, though a small one.

Replacements deserve high priority only if a very small change can convert an almost right product into one that fits the ideal business design.

What distinguishes a replacement from a development is that it represents a different idea of what the market is and what it wants, or a different exploitation of the company's knowledge. A new packaging material is a development – no matter how difficult technologically it might be to design and to produce it. A new packaging concept, shipping on pallets or in container bodies which fit on railway flatcars as well as on highway trucks, is a new idea and a replacement. In the General Motors redesign by Alfred P. Sloan, Jr, the replacements were the three cars that were revamped in everything but name: the old low-priced Chevrolet, the Oakland (later the Pontiac), and the Oldsmobile. These cars had customer acceptance and a dealer organization. They had the basic design. What they did not have was a clear idea of their function and place in the market, the right pricing policy, and management. For a downtown department store in the United States the suburban shopping centres were essentially replacements; they were ways to make the essential strengths of the department store – its reputation and its merchandising knowledge – available where the customers shopped.

A replacement should never present great technical difficulty. It should arise out of the recognition: 'Now we suddenly understand what is wrong with this product, this market, this activity. Now we suddenly understand what we have done wrong, or failed to do.' What changes is much less the product itself – if it is not almost right one should not waste time and effort on it – than the way the business itself sees, presents and uses the product.

Innovation is the design and development of something new, as yet unknown and not in existence, which will establish a new economic configuration out of the old, known, existing elements. It will give these elements an entirely new economic dimension. It is the missing link between having a number of disconnected elements, each marginally effective, and an integrated system of great power.

It is this 'systems' aspect of innovation that is invoked when we say that the men like Siemens or Edison created a new industry. All the elements were there, except one. Adding this one new element created an entirely new economic capacity. There are many other examples:

Sears Roebuck built its business on the innovation of a 'money-back-and-no-questions-asked' guarantee to the farm customers. All the ingredients of a successful mail-order business existed. What was lacking was the simple element of confidence in the customer.

IBM similarly created the computer industry by innovating the concept of programming as a distinct function which bridged the gap between the technically highly complex machine and the technically untrained potential customers, and which yet could be learned by high-school graduates in a short time.

Sloan's innovation was the idea of an automobile company supplying the entire market in a planned and organized fashion where formerly General Motors – and all the others – had seen themselves as producers of individual makes each trying to appeal to all the potential customers.

American Motors innovated the idea of the 'compact', that is the smallest car that would still give adequate room and performance to people used to big cars.

Innovation is not invention or discovery. It may require either – and often does. But its focus is not knowledge but performance – and in a business this means economic performance. Its essence is conceptual rather than technical or scientific. The characteristic of the innovator is the ability to envisage as a system what to others are unrelated, separate elements. Innovation is not the better the bigger it is. On the contrary, it is the better the smaller it can be. It is, to say it again, the successful attempt to find and to provide the smallest missing part that will convert already existing elements – knowledge, products, customer demand, markets – into a new and much more productive whole.

To find the areas where innovation would create maximum opportunities, one asks: What is lacking to make effective what is already possible? What one small step would transform our economic results? What small change would alter the capacity of the whole of our resources?

To describe the need is not to satisfy it. But describing the need gives a specification for the desirable results. Whether they are likely to be obtained can then be decided. Innovation is applicable to finding business potential and to making the future. But its first application is as a strategy for making today fully effective, and for bringing the existing business closer to the ideal business.

STAFFING FOR PERFORMANCE

The crux of a programme of action is the allocation of resources, and especially the staffing decisions. Until they have been made and put into effect, nothing has really been *done*.

The one principle for the deployment of the scarcest and most productive resource – high-calibre people – is maximization of resources. Few businesses have resources of a calibre comparable to that of the four older Rothschild sons. But every business should follow the Rothschild example – if it wants results.

First-class people must always be allocated to major opportunities, to the areas of greatest possible return for each unit of effort. And first-class opportunities must always be staffed with people of superior ability and performance. If there are no resources available for major opportunities one must build them. One never tries to exploit major opportunities with anything but high-grade resources. One never assigns high-grade resources to anything but major opportunities, however. And one does not create resources for secondary opportunities.

To follow these principles in practice, however, is not easy. There are, first, the 'Kalmann Rothschilds' – the 'members of the family in good standing' whose faithful service entitles them to be taken care of even though they lack the necessary ability. It is always cheaper to give them a sinecure than to entrust them with a major opportunity. In a sinecure they cost only their salary. In charge of a major opportunity they may waste the potential return from a new big business.

Equally unpopular is the decision to leave secondary opportunities to fend for themselves. Yet unless one is ruthless, the first-rate opportunities starve to death.

But the greatest temptation is to diffuse first-rate resources rather than to concentrate them: it is so easy to avoid painful priority decisions by asking a strong man to be 'available for support and advice' to a weak one. 'It should, after all, take only a day or two of his time, once in a while' is the standard excuse. But in no time at all the few really good men will do nothing but bolster weak men and secondary opportunities. Strength, to be effective, has to be concentrated. And any major opportunity is a challenge demanding undivided attention and dedication.

It is indeed so painful to staff for performance that managers should impose on themselves the discipline of what the psychologists call the 'forced-choice method'.

A list of major opportunities is drawn up, with each opportunity assigned a ranking. Here is the first forced choice – for each opportunity has to be ranked without ambiguity. The same procedure is followed with respect to first-rate people and staff groups – again ranking them by forced choice. Then to the highest-ranking opportunity is allocated all the high-ranking human resources it requires. The next-ranking opportunity comes next, then the third-ranking one, and so on. A lower-ranking opportunity is never staffed at the expense of a higher-ranking one.

The ranking of opportunities and of people becomes the real decision in this method; the rest follows.

Staffing decisions are the crucial decision. They decide whether the business has a programme for effectiveness or only a scrap of paper.

10

Finding Business Potential

'Opportunity is where you find it,' says an old proverb. It does not say: '. . . where it finds you.' Luck, chance and catastrophe affect business as they do all human endeavours. But luck never built a business. Prosperity and growth come only to the business that systematically finds and exploits its potential. No matter how successfully a business organizes itself for the challenges and opportunities of the present, it will still be far below its optimum performance. Its potential is always greater than its realized actuality.

Dangers and weaknesses indicate where to look for business potential. To convert them from problems into opportunities brings extraordinary returns. And sometimes all that is needed to accomplish this transformation is a change in the attitude of the executives.

Three questions will bring out the hidden potential of a business:

What are the restraints and limitations that make the business vulnerable, impede its full effectiveness, and hold down its economic results?

What are the imbalances of the business?

What are we afraid of, what do we see as a threat to this business – and how can we use it as an opportunity?

VULNERABILITY AS AN OPPORTUNITY

Why is a particular business – or industry – extremely vulnerable to minor economic fluctuations? What makes its products incapable of meeting competition from new or different products? Is there a single factor that restrains the full realization of its economic capacity?

While these questions can rarely be answered offhand, most executives have a pretty good notion of the restraints, vulnerabilities and limitations of their company and industry. The trouble is that the questions are rarely asked. Executives tend to assume that nothing can be done to change the situation. 'If we knew how to overcome the limitations of our process, we would have done so long ago' is a common attitude. This process as it stands may indeed represent the best current knowledge. But it is emphatically not true that nothing can be done about it.

The development of the American steel industry in the period after World War II illustrates such a vulnerability and how it affects an industry.

Shortly after the end of World War II one of the major steel companies commissioned a group of young economists experienced in the analysis of industry structure and markets to make a forecast of steel demand in the United States. It expected the usual projection of growth trends relating steel demands to national income and production. The emphasis in the report was not on the projection, however, but on an analysis of the underlying assumptions. Much to the surprise of the steel company executives, the economists questioned the assumption that steel is of necessity the basic industrial material of a modern society. Other materials were increasingly capable of fulfilling many of the functions for which steel had been bought – and the then existing steelmaking process had such cost limitations as to make dubious its capacity to compete.

The steelmaking process, developed in the middle of the nineteenth century, requires high temperature to be created three times, only to be quenched three times. It further requires moving heavy loads over considerable distances, and handling them in a particularly difficult form; namely, as molten and very hot metal. The two most expensive things to do, however – whether one talks physics or economics – are creating temperatures and moving and handling. All the costs of a mechanical batch process were therefore built into the economic structure of the steel industry. Other materials, especially plastics, aluminium, glass and concrete had the much more favourable economics of heat-conserving flow processes. And these other materials were reaching a state in which they could give satisfactory performance in a number of major end-uses for which steel had traditionally been the only available material – from construction work to packaging.

At the same time, the report went on, there was mounting evidence that the basic limitations of the steelmaking process were being tackled. Though until then only minor improvements and modifications, these new approaches might, within a fairly short period, result in fundamental changes in technology.

When the steel company commissioned the study it had expected recommendations for rapid expansion of its capacity. Indeed, several of the more conservative executives had opposed the study as likely to encourage wild over-expansion. But the conclusions of the study were entirely different.

The economists came up with two recommendations. One called for extreme caution in expanding capacity until such time as basic changes in the economics of the steelmaking process would become available. Till then, additional capacity should be built only for products and markets in which steel would have at least a 25 per cent price advantage compared to any potentially competitive material. The second recommendation called for an accelerated research programme focused on basic process innovation.

The company executives who had ordered the study, promptly dismissed it as 'typical academic nonsense'. But it proved to be prophetic.

The American steel industry has pushed an expansion programme in the post-war years based on the old assumptions and has built a good deal of expensive capacity applying the old processes. The demand was indeed there – but far less for steel than for its new competitors which have made sizeable inroads in markets that used to be steel's very own (and they may make yet bigger inroads should fibre glass become competitive with steel sheet in automobile bodies, for instance). The European and the Soviet steel industries blithely followed the Americans, and also expanded on the assumption that the traditional relationship between steel demand and economic activity must continue. In the meantime, however, the technological changes – which steelmakers all considered 'impossible' as recently as 1950 – have been coming in: continuous casting, for instance, and the high-oxygen converter which materially improves heat utilization and speed and cuts down on moving costs.

As a result a good deal of the investments in steel expansion made before 1955 (that is, the bulk of the post-war investment in the United States and Russia) will probably never earn an adequate return. Even Mr Khrushchev had to admit in 1962 that he had planned for far more steel plant than he could actually use. This capacity will either be inadequately used; or it will produce steel at a cost well above what the market will pay. But steel capacity built after 1955, when the new process technologies became available, should not only restore the competitive position of steel in a great many markets but should also be able to earn high returns both on fairly low output and on fairly low price.

This story is given here in such detail because it illustrates the essentials:

The vulnerabilities and restraints are as a rule well known or easily ascertained; the young economists who made the study knew little about steel or its technology and went by what the steel men themselves told them.

Any basic change proposed to overcome the vulnerability seems to the people in an industry so unlikely as to be impossible. But it is often in train while everybody is still proclaiming that it cannot happen.

Whenever a restraint or vulnerability of this kind can be changed, the economic results are likely to be substantial. Such a restraint therefore represents a major opportunity. Overcoming such a restraint almost always requires systematic innovation; that is, analysis to define the new capacity or knowledge and systematic work on its development.

There are three major areas in which restraint should be looked for: the process – as in the steel industry; the economics of the industry; and the economics of the market.

1. Any process which results in both a high break-even point in terms of volume and a high break-even point in terms of price makes a business (or industry) vulnerable. Ideally, of course, a business should have both low volume and low price break-even points. But at the least it should not be flexible in its volume as well as in its prices. The business that runs at a loss unless it runs at 98 per cent capacity *and* at boom-levels of price is highly vulnerable.

Wherever such a condition is found – and it is unfortunately fairly common – the process has been over-engineered to the detriment of its economics. It has been engineered for best physical performance rather than for best economic performance. Examples are, for instance, some of the 'most modern' paper mills in which high-speed finishing has been integrated at great cost in ingenuity and money with the high-speed paper-forming process – with the result that the machine can indeed produce incredible quantities of finished paper, but of one kind and grade only. A minor change in demand could make it uneconomical.

Rather more complex are the process-economics of ocean shipping, discussed in Chapter 5. Ocean shipping could actually be a major growth industry, both in tonnage and in earnings. International trade is growing rapidly; and the ocean-going ship is still the main carrier. But since for generations naval architects have concentrated on the performance of a ship at sea instead of in port, they have actually made port-work (the major cost element) more difficult and time-consuming. As a result of the wrong emphasis in process-design, ocean-going shipping is not growing today. Though heavily subsidized it is threatened by the same fate that has been overtaking the railroads: replacement by another carrier as the mainstay of transportation; in this case, the air-freighter. That the ship is not inherently inferior is shown by the success of those ocean-going freighters which have been designed for loading and unloading rather than for high-speed or low-cost performance on the high seas, e.g., the specialized bulk carriers such as the petroleum tanker, the ore boat, or the banana boat.

Since prevention is easier than cure, the balance between economic and engineering performance should always be worked out in the design of a new process, particularly in automation. Automation, if properly engineered, should make the process more flexible; that is, capable of both optimum economic performance under optimum conditions – high demand for a standardized product, for instance – and optimum economic performance under less-than-optimum conditions, such as lower demand or sharply fluctuating product and order mixes. Instead a great deal of automation repeats the mistake of the paper-machine designers and sacrifices economic performance and flexibility to top speed in turning out today's product. Such equipment is actually obsolete the day it starts running; for today's product never stays the right product long. Today's automation miracle becomes tomorrow's vulnerability unless the economics of the process are engineered into it; that is, unless the inherent capacity of automation to make flexibility and diversity economical is fully utilized.

2. To illustrate restraint and vulnerability in the economics of an industry, paper again serves as an example:

Like steel, paper has been a multi-purpose material, and even more than steel has tended to grow several times as fast as the total economy. As with steel, however, a host of new materials have come in, each better suited than paper for one particular purpose or application. And like steel, paper is becoming expensive in comparison to the newcomers.

The papermaking process uses no more than a quarter of the tree. Half of the wood in the tree is left behind in the forest, and another quarter is thrown away in the form of bark, leaves, small branches and organic chemicals such as lignin. Yet the papermakers have to pay for the whole tree. As a result, pulp, the raw material of papermaking is expensive compared for instance with the raw materials from which plastics are made, which are usually by-products of petroleum refining and virtually free of cost. If the paper industry could convert into saleable products the three-quarters of the tree that is today being wasted, paper would again become cheap. Otherwise, paper, now a multi-purpose material, may find itself confined to a few uses, and the paper industry may shrink rather than grow with the economy.

The papermaker will immediately point out that no one knows as yet how to use the three-quarters of the tree that is thrown away. He will point out further that strenuous efforts have been made by the paper industry to develop the chemical utilization of wood, so far however with meagre results. He will, in other words, point out that he is not to blame for the situation – and he is right. But that it may not yet be possible to do something about such a fundamental restraint does not alter the fact that it exists and that it may endanger the future of an industry. It does not alter the fact that removal of the restraint would have extraordinary impact on the economic potential of an industry. It does not alter the fact, in brief, that here is an area in which an industry has to keep on working, no matter how frustrating the prospect seems to be. For when the change comes, it is likely to come fast.

3. Finally, the restraint – and the vulnerability it causes – may

lie in market structure and economics that are at odds with the structure and economics of the company or industry.

In Chapter 6 above, one such restraint was mentioned: the apparently irrational behaviour of the customer; that is, behaviour that seems contrary not only to the interest of the supplier but to that of the customer as well. But equally serious vulnerabilities can be found in technological or economic systems which prevent customer-interest from becoming a source of business and profit for the supplier.

An example is residential building. In the American residential market the price differential between a new, cheap, one-family house and a medium-priced one is only 25 per cent or so. The quality differential, however, is enormous. The cheap home deteriorates fast. In a few years – usually well before the buyers have finished paying for it – they either move on to a better one or have lost most of their investment and are condemned to living in a deteriorating home in a deteriorating neighbourhood. Slums are not made by the slum dwellers. They are made when new homes are built in such a manner that they are doomed to a fast decline. The trouble is, of course, that the young couple who first buy a home have only enough money for the cheapest available building unit. This, today, means one that will deteriorate pretty fast.*

The restraint here lies in the traditional way of building a house. What is needed is what might be called an add-on house. The young family, starting out life together, should be able to buy the core of a home of good quality and yet of low price, to which they can add units and features as their income grows or as they pay off the original home mortgage. Thus it would be possible for them to upgrade their home constantly and to increase its value. This would eliminate – or at least greatly lessen – the incentive for the successful families to move out of the neighbourhood in which they began and thus convert it into a low-class neighbourhood and eventually a slum. It would, at the same time, create the desirable 'mixed' neighbourhood of fair-sized homes owned and occupied by older

---

* I am conscious of gross oversimplification of a complex problem. Land use is at least as important a factor in real estate values and city development as is building construction. And many other factors enter the picture. I am only trying, however, to illustrate the restraint analysis, not to give an exposition of the problems of modern city planning.

and fairly prosperous people, and small homes for the younger and less prosperous. Yet each home would have substantial quality and would be capable of constant upgrading.

This is obviously difficult to bring about. It may be impossible. But the construction industry had better work out some such solution. It is bound to suffer if housing continues to become more expensive and yet increasingly prone to deterioration.

Such vulnerability is not confined to businesses or industries making and selling a product; it can be found in service industries as well.

The American commercial bank (like all commercial banks) derives its profits from the use of the customer's deposits. At the same time the services with which it competes for deposits are aimed at enabling the customer to operate with a minimum of cash and, therefore, with a minimum of deposits. The more value it gives its customers, the less well it is likely to do itself. The commercial banks get paid, in other words, for the exact opposite of what the customer really buys. The customer buys money management which enables him to function with the least amount of idle cash. But banks make more money the more idle cash the customer keeps on deposit. Typically, the greatest skill and virtuosity in the industry goes into managing this internal contradiction. The heroes of commercial banking are the men who can best advise customers on their money management, while at the same time persuading them to keep the largest possible deposit balance with the bank for the longest possible time.

One solution might be to get paid for what is value to the customer – that is, money management – on a fee basis.

For years any suggestion to this effect was greeted with derision by the bankers. If there was one thing they knew, it was that no bank would dream of offering such a service and no customer would dream of accepting it. Yet this is exactly the arrangement that one of the country's biggest and most conservative banks, the Morgan Guaranty Trust Company in New York, has worked out with one of the country's most conservative large corporations, Gillette Razor (as disclosed in the autumn of 1963).

The most promising area of potential is the built-in restraint of a business. But to convert restraint into opportunity demands innovation.

TURNING WEAKNESSES INTO STRENGTHS

Perfect balance in a business exists only on the organization chart. A living business is always in a state of imbalance, growing here here and shrinking there, overdoing one thing and neglecting another.

But many businesses are in chronic imbalance; they need productive resources way beyond any results they can produce. 'We are just a small company with fifteen million dollars in sales; but we need a national sales force, national promotion and national distribution' is the complaint of one company. Another says: 'We have to maintain a solid-state physics laboratory to match General Electric's work in the field' – and yet the field in which the company operates is narrow and highly specialized.

Such imbalance is a serious weakness; it may threaten a company's existence. The total cost structure of any business is likely to be scaled to the size of its largest resource. Support costs tend to be geared to the productive efforts that need to be supported rather than to the available results. The company with the large research force in advanced solid-state physics, for instance, provides its physicists with facilities, buildings, equipment, library services, and so on, that compare favourably with those of the General Electric Company; otherwise it risks losing its best men to the big competitor. The large national sales force for a $15-million volume will demand as much in the way of accounting, order-handling, supervision and training as if the company handled $150 million a year of business. Total costs, in other words, tend to be proportionate to the costs of the largest needed productive effort.

But results, of course, are proportionate to the revenues; that is, to volume.

Where the imbalance in efforts is in support activities, in policing activities, or in waste, the cure is to cut out whatever causes the imbalance. The principle of least effort for support and policing costs, developed in Chapter 5, applies here, as does the rule to eliminate waste efforts altogether.

But when the imbalance lies in disproportionately large productive efforts, it often indicates a major unused potential. To exploit this potential always requires major changes in the nature and structure of the business.

Typical areas of imbalance with disproportionately large productive resources incapable of producing adequate results within the existing business are marketing and research and development.

Here is an example of an imbalance in marketing resources – together with the specific course of action taken to convert the potential into performance.

The company with the large national sales force employed to sell $15 million worth of merchandise across the United States could not materially cut back its selling efforts without destroying its business. But the volume could also not support the 150 technically trained salesmen. An analysis showed that profitable operations required average sales per salesmen of half a million a year as against the prevailing average of $100,000. The solution was a radical redefinition of the business as a distributor rather than as a manufacturer. An intensive search was made for other small manufacturers making similar goods similarly requiring national distribution. To them the company offered its services far below the sales cost of manufacturers. Five years later the company distributed with the same sales force some $100 million worth of merchandise. Only one-fifth were its own goods; the rest were the products of seven other non-competing manufacturers, each selling less than $20 million worth but getting the full benefits of a sales organization geared to a $100-million volume.

Imbalance between research and development resources and the business they produce is equally costly and equally a major opportunity.

Costs of research and development sky-rocketed when a medium-sized glass company began to supply glass to the electronics industry for a variety of components. The increase was so great as to threaten the profitability of the entire business – even though glass for electronic purposes was a relatively small part of the entire product line. The company at first considered withdrawing from the electronics market; but a market study showed that electronics was a major growth industry and that its use of glass was likely to grow twice as fast as the industry itself. (This was in 1952.) The company then tried to find out why its electronic industry sales required such exorbitant technological efforts and found that its research people in effect were doing the entire technical job for the electronics customer. The essential knowledge was not electronics but glass; and performance of the finished component depended primarily on the glass, its quality and design. In terms of money the glass was almost insignificant in the finished component; in terms of technological effort it dominated – but the company was not getting paid for the contribution.

The solution here was to integrate forward into electronics manufacturing. Components that are essentially electronic applications of glass technology are now being made by the company. Dollar volume and profits are several times what they would be if the company only furnished the glass. And this means more than adequate utilization of the technological effort needed.

The move was, of course, fought within the company with the old argument. 'We cannot go into competition with our own customers.' As often happens, the outside business with old customers has gone up – if only because the company now can give better service and design better glass than before.

Not only marketing and technological resources but every productive resource can be out of balance – a serious danger if unattended, but also an opportunity for growth.

An example is an instalment finance company founded by one of the smaller American automobile companies. Financing the purchase of automobiles, it has to operate nation-wide with branch offices in all big cities. But confined to the product of one of the smaller automobile manufacturers, it simply could not generate the volume of instalment finance needed to carry its local administrative expenses. With a total volume of $400 million of instalment finance a year, it looked like a very big company. Actually it was too small for its specific productive resources, the ability to control and manage a highly specialized instalment finance business. The solution was to become the instalment finance company for a fairly large number of even smaller but still nationally distributing manufacturers of durable consumer goods sold on the instalment plan. With its overhead largely paid for by automobile finance, the company could offer outsiders attractive terms and soon had its volume up to $600 million or so, at which point it became profitable.

The unbalanced productive resources need not be within the legal framework of the business itself. They can be within the economic process but outside the legal (and accounting) structure.

The shift from small, specialized retailer to mass-distributor typically creates such an imbalance. Many American manufacturers of nationally distributed goods for mass-consumption still have three-quarters of their distribution in small retail stores, whereas three-quarters of consumer purchases are in mass-distribution outlets. This inevitably creates an imbalance. On the one hand, the manufacturer has to maintain a distribution expense he can ill-afford, since he has to service a large number of small stores which are at best marginally productive. On the other hand, he does not reach his market. His marketing efforts are out of balance with their possible results.

This may seem elementary. But only a cost analysis that takes the price paid by the ultimate consumer as cost basis will bring out that distribution costs are disproportionately high. The conventional analysis, in which costs are defined as the expenses within a given legal unit rather than as the expenses of an economic process, tends to hide such an imbalance in distribution costs and distributive channels. This imbalance itself is fairly easy to correct, but it may escape detection for many years.

In the United States this imbalance has led to the sale of a large number of businesses by frustrated and baffled owners. They could not figure out why their formerly profitable business had ceased to produce earnings. Yet the purchasers restored profitability fast by redirecting distribution into mass channels. In Europe (and increasingly in Japan) the same development is taking place now. The consumers are switching from small, specialized, low-turnover retail stores to large, fast-turnover mass-distribution. Many manufacturers, however, maintain their old distributive channels. As these cease to produce results they intensify their marketing and selling efforts which, however, only aggravates the imbalance. Ultimately they sell out to someone who understands the change and sees in it an opportunity for selling more at less cost and with greater effectiveness.

Sometimes supporting activities have to be maintained at such high level of effort and competence that they cause imbalance.

The best example I know is a large company in the processed

food, hotel and catering businesses. It requires many auxiliary services: laundry, for instance, for its hotels and restaurants, and trucking for its processed-foods distribution. Each of these services has to operate at a high level of performance. Each requires fairly substantial capital investment and has to be maintained at a level sufficient to carry the peak load. Each, therefore, is almost certain to become disproportionately large and expensive.

The company has a simple rule. Support activities that require knowledge and competence similar to the businesses they serve – the laundry service, for instance, or trucking – are developed into regular, profit-making businesses with outside customers. The laundry has become a large commercial laundry. The trucking service is a leader in its area. Both do four to five times as much work for outside customers as they do for the company's businesses. Both, as a result, have to be able to prove themselves in competitive performance.

This solution, however, requires not only a constant search for opportunities. It also requires the self-discipline not to develop businesses from support activities that can be run on the least-effort principle – let alone from those that do not fit in with the main business of the company.

In the food and catering company of the present illustration, two rules are strictly applied: support activities that need not be run at a high level of size or excellence are kept small. Even if capable of becoming profitable businesses they are not enlarged beyond the bare minimum needed for internal operations. The rule applies to the printing shop, for instance, even though it could well be made into a substantial business. And, furthermore, support activities that need to be developed in size or excellence without, however, fitting in with the company's general business are developed until they are substantial, profitable concerns. Then they are sold off – and the company becomes their customer. This was done, for instance, with a department designing and building stores and restaurants; it is now one of the leading architects for commercial structures.

THE BUSINESS OF THE WRONG SIZE

The most important cases of imbalance are businesses that are the wrong size – usually too small – for the market they have to serve or for the management they need.

The European Common Market created such imbalance for many medium-sized, family-owned businesses. Perfectly adequate, perhaps, to supply their own limited national market, they found themselves short of the products, the capital, the marketing resources, or the management to compete successfully against the industrial giants in a market of 180 million people. This explains the wave of mergers in the last decade between such family companies across national boundaries in Europe, and the large number of partnership agreements, co-operative marketing agreements or research pools into which European family companies – traditionally suspicious of any outsider – have entered since the Common Market first started. A similar development is going on in Japan where small family-owned businesses find themselves unable to cope with a mass-market of almost 100 million customers. And – though on a much smaller scale – a parallel development has been taking place in California since World World II abolished the economic isolation in which high freight costs had kept the West Coast market.

Any major change in the market – and especially in its size and complexity – is likely to create an imbalance between the size of the smaller or medium-sized firm and the demands made on it. Like all imbalances this too is a hidden opportunity; but the solution is not normally to add to the existing business. It is merger, acquisition, partnership, or joint venture – that is, fundamental change of business structure and usually (though not inevitably) change of financial structure and ownership.

This is also the only solution that converts into opportunity the imbalance between the size of a business and the management it needs.

Management too is a productive resource. Serious imbalance in the size – and with it, the cost – of management, is therefore serious under-utilization of a valuable, expensive and scarce resource. Though the company needs first-rate managers, it can neither pay them adequately nor offer enough challenge and achievement. If it succeeds in attracting the kind of man it needs – or in developing him – it soon loses him again. The business is thus stunted and may even be destroyed in the end. If, however, the imbalance is treated as an opportunity, it can become the source of rapid growth, both in volume and profitability.

Sometimes a small or medium-sized business overloads itself with expensive and unneeded management.

Typically such a business goes in for the latest management fads. When 'human relations' are in season, it hires psychologists, social workers, and personnel experts and puts everybody through 'leadership training'. Two years later everybody talks 'operations research' and attends management-science seminars. A computer big enough to handle all the paper-work of the federal government is considered barely adequate for the payroll of a company employing 250 people.

In such a situation, one can scale management down to the size appropriate to the needs of the business.

But there is often genuine need for complex management in a company that lacks the business to support it.

A large engineering company maintains that a technically advanced business in the American civilian market requires a sales volume of $15 million to pay for its management and technical efforts. Most of the businesses of the company require substantial capital investment in large, highly mechanized plants, continuing research and development work, specialized selling, and a good deal of technical service. Even so, the figure is probably quite high. Independent companies in the same fields compete and prosper on a volume of no more that $10 or 12 million. In other highly technical fields – for example, in chemical specialties – companies with a sales volume of $5 to 7 million do well and have leadership in a market. Altogether, sales volume is probably a good deal less important than value added (that is, sales less purchased materials and parts); on that basis a chemical company with $5 million turnover using cheap raw materials (crude oil or sand, for instance) might actually be a bigger business than an engineering company of $15 million sales with 70 per cent purchased materials and parts.

The economical size for businesses varies with the industry; with the maturity of the technology (in new technologies small size may be both economical and advantageous); with the market and its structure; and so on. But the business of the wrong size pays a heavy penalty. It pays the full costs of the larger size, but gets only the benefit of the smaller size – and sometimes not even that.

In some industries a business must either be quite small and serve a distinct segment of the market or else be very big. In the American soap industry, for instance, small businesses are viable and prosperous serving one narrow geographic area in which they have leadership, or a specific class of customers – for instance, hospitals. But the next possible size in the soap industry is the giant national brands, nationally promoted and distributed. A soap business in between cannot prosper, probably cannot even survive.

There have long been very big European automobile companies: Fiat, the British Ford, Opel and, lately, Volkswagen. But quite small companies assembling a few thousand cars a year from purchased parts could survive and prosper as long as the market was small. But with Europe going through the automotive revolution in record time, a consolidation of the industry into a fairly small number of very big companies is now clearly in the offing. Even the many medium-sized companies with well-established names and a loyal following cannot, it seems, survive; everything smaller than the giant is too small.

A recent book, *Corporations in Crisis,** mentions two companies that had to sell out to big concerns – not because they failed but because they were so successful that they grew to an untenable in-between size. Stavid Engineering, successful as a small specialty designer with a few million dollars worth of business a year, grew to a volume of $10 million and found that it had to have the management of a $20 million business – without the means to attain that volume. It is now a division of Lockheed Aircraft. Similarly, success of its V-107 helicopter forced small and prosperous Piasecki Helicopter Corporation into an uneconomical size. It sold out to big Boeing Aircraft.

Sometimes the right solution for the company that is in-between in size is to retrench to a smaller, economical volume.

A small manufacturer of plumbers' equipment and tools did well with a volume of $8 million a year, supplying the tri-state area around Chicago (Illinois, Wisconsin, Indiana). His goods being heavy, he enjoyed a distinct freight advantage within a short radius around his plant. When he branched out into a wider territory his sales quickly went up to $20 million. But he

* Richard Austin Smith (New York: Doubleday, 1963).

lost so much on these additional sales – for to be competitive he had to absorb freight charges to outlying areas – that he was forced into bankruptcy. Retrenchment to his original territory restored his economic health. In this industry to be anything but a small supplier of a local market requires a multiplant operation in many locations – probably with a minimum volume close to $50 million a year.

The most important case is, however, that of the business that is below the minimum size. It is marginal, no matter how good its products. The money that should be invested in growth is needed instead to support the extra burden of management, research, sales efforts, and so on. But unless the company grows it will not be able to generate the money it needs.

The only solution to this vicious circle is to jump. It is a quantum jump; one cannot be between two sizes but must move in one step from one size to the next. Gradual growth from within is not possible, as a rule. Only sale of the company, acquisition of another company in the same industry, or merger will produce a business of the needed size.

'WHAT ARE WE AFRAID OF?'

There are hidden opportunities in developments that seem to threaten a business or an industry.

As late as 1950 the American railroads refused to accept that passenger automobile, truck and airplane were here to stay. They considered it unthinkable that railroads could be displaced as the backbone of the country's transportation system. The new means of transportation were a threat – not only to the railroads but, they argued, to the nation, its security and prosperity.

It was not until well into the 1960s that the railroads began to realize that this threat could also be seen as opportunity. With alternate means of transportation available, they could concentrate on what they do best and most profitably: long-distance hauling of bulk commodities. The car, the truck and the bus allow the railroads to drop branch lines and unprofitable service to small communities. They ease the deeply-ingrained fear of railroad monopoly and thereby make politically acceptable mergers of competing lines and elimination of costly service duplication.

An almost immediate result of this change in attitude was the reconquest of a business the railroads had given up for lost twenty-five years earlier: long-distance hauling of new automobiles. As long as the railroads viewed the truck as 'abnormal' they could not conceive of any other method of carrying automobiles than the small, closed box car – even though the trucks had all along been carrying automobiles on open double-decker trailers. To ship two cars – a normal box-car load – on the railroad cost as much as to carry six cars by truck. As soon as the railroads accepted the fact that the truck was here to stay, they saw the opportunity to carry eight or ten automobiles on one double-decker trailer – and to pull a great many of these automobile-carrying trailers behind one locomotive. Within eighteen months the railroads had recaptured the bulk of long-distance automobile haulage.

Similar developments are making grain, coal and iron-ore shipments again profitable for the railroad – as bulk shipments, in bulk carriers, and at bulk rates. The principal lines may even again become prosperous and healthy businesses as a result of their basic change of attitude – though they waited far too long before they accepted the inevitable and attempted to co-operate with it.

Here are some further examples:

The American life insurance companies used to be the main savings channel for the community. In the years after World War II, the public, in its new affluence, began to put decreasing shares of its savings into life insurance (without, however, actually reducing the dollar amounts of life insurance bought). Most of the companies saw in this a serious threat to be fought by publicity campaigns aimed at warning the American family of the dangers of the new investment media such as common stock. Only one company – significantly enough one that had never before been prominent in the life insurance field – saw in this an opportunity. It purchased a mutual investment trust and began to sell its certificates together with its life insurance policies, thus offering the customer a balanced investment and a one-package approach to his financial planning. It soon achieved a rapid growth rate, well beyond that of the industry as a whole.

The great majority of American department stores at first fought the discount store as 'unethical'. When this did not work, one after the other of the major department store chains joined the parade and opened discount stores of its own. The results have mostly been poor; department stores do not know how to run a discount operation. One major store chain, however, took an entirely different tack. This chain has not opened discount stores and does not intend to do so. Instead it has upgraded its own stores. In every city in which it operates, it has become the quality store for the mass market. It concentrates on high quality lines, especially apparel of good design, fashionable though conservative. 'We want our customers to buy little Susie's pyjamas at the discount house in her neighbourhood,' an executive of the chain said. 'This way the mother will have more money to spend with us when she comes to buy the one good party frock for Susie's first dance.'

There is also the example of a major paper company which, for years, bemoaned the threat of plastics without doing anything about it. It finally forced itself to look upon plastics as an opportunity. As a result it expanded its investment in packaging and container manufacture to take advantage of the trend: its packaging and container subsidiaries are as willing to use plastics as any other material. To the extent to which they become major factors in the packaging market, the parent company benefits from the trend toward plastics, rather than being threatened by it.

Sometimes a business needs to ask: 'What compromises with what we claim to be harmful to our business are we already making? Are they actually harmful? Or do we benefit?'

It was this question that made a leading soft-drink bottler in the United States take a new look at its market. For years the company had actively campaigned against low-calorie drinks as a fad. Management was convinced that these drinks (which are not based on a special formula or a secret ingredient) were a threat to its own branded product – which is rather high in calories. But while more and more of the company's bottlers took on low-calorie drinks, they also sold more of the old, standard beverage – the diet drinks built a market for the old product rather than cutting into it. It took management several years before it accepted the facts. Now the company itself is making, promoting and selling low-calorie drinks of its own – and its sales of both the old and the new line have greatly increased.

11

Making the Future Today

We know only two things about the future:

    It cannot be known.

    It will be different from what exists now and from what
we now expect.

These assertions are not particularly new or particularly striking. But they have far-reaching implications.

1. Any attempt to base today's actions and commitments on *predictions* of *future events* is futile. The best we can hope to do is to anticipate *future effects of events* which have already irrevocably happened.

2. But precisely because the future is going to be different and cannot be predicted, it is possible to make the unexpected and unpredicted come to pass. To try to make the future happen is risky; but it is rational activity. And it is less risky than coasting along on the comfortable assumption that nothing is going to change, less risky than following a prediction as to what 'must' happen or what is 'most probable'.

Business these last ten or twenty years has accepted the need to work systematically on making the future. But long-range planning does not – and cannot – aim at the elimination of risks and uncertainties. That is not given to mortal man. The one thing he can try is to find, and occasionally to create, the right risk and to exploit uncertainty. The purpose of the work on making the future is not to decide what should be done tomorrow, but what should be done today to have a tomorrow.

The deliberate commitment of present resources to an unknown and unknowable future is the specific function of the entrepreneur in the term's original meaning. J. B. Say, the great French economist who coined the word around the year 1800, used it to describe the man who attracts capital locked up in the unproductive past (e.g., in marginal land) and commits it to the risk of making a different future. English economists such as Adam Smith with their focus on the trader saw efficiency as the central economic function. Say, however, rightly stressed the creation of risk and the exploitation of the discontinuity between today and tomorrow as the wealth-producing economic activities.

Now we are learning slowly how to do this work systematically and with direction and control. The starting point is the realization that there are two different – though complementary – approaches:

Finding and exploiting the time lag between the appearance of a discontinuity in economy and society and its full impact – one might call this *anticipation of a future that has already happened.*

Imposing on the as yet unborn future a new ideal which tries to give direction and shape to what is to come. This one might call *making the future happen.*

THE FUTURE THAT HAS ALREADY HAPPENED

There is a time lag between a major social, economic, or cultural event and its full impact. A sharp rise or a sharp drop in the birthrate will not have an effect on the size of the available labour force for fifteen to twenty years. But the change has already happened. Only catastrophe – destructive war, famine, or pandemic – could prevent its impact tomorrow.

These are the opportunities of the future that has already happened. They might therefore be called a potential. But unlike the potential discussed in the last chapter, the future that has already happened is not within the present business; it is outside: a change in society, knowledge, culture, industry, or economic structure.

It is, moreover, a major change rather than a trend, a break in the pattern rather than a variation within it. There is, of course, considerable uncertainty and risk in committing resources to anticipation. But the risk is limited. We cannot really know how fast the impact will occur. But that it will occur we can say with a high degree of assurance; and we can, to a useful extent, describe it.

There is a lot we cannot anticipate regarding the impact of a change in birthrate on the labour force: how large a proportion of the women will be in the labour force, for instance; how many of today's young children will stay in school well beyond age fourteen or sixteen; where the future jobs will be, and how many; and so forth. But one can say with assurance: 'This is the largest the labour force can be a decade or two hence – for to be in it a person has to have been born by now.' One can equally say: 'That Latin America in the last generation has changed from a rural to an urban society is a fact – and it is bound to have long-range impact.'

Fundamental knowledge has to be available today to be able to serve us ten or fifteen years hence. In the mid-nineteenth century one could only speculate about the consequences for the economy of Michael Faraday's discoveries in electricity. A good many of the speculations were undoubtedly wide of the mark. But that this breakthrough into an entirely new field of energy would have major impact could be said with some certainty.

Major cultural changes too operate over a fairly long period. This is particularly true of the subtlest but most pervasive cultural change: a change in people's awareness. It is by no means certain that the underdeveloped countries will succeed in rapidly developing themselves. On the contrary, it is probable that only a few will succeed, and that even these few will go through difficult times and suffer severe crises. But that the peoples of Latin America, Asia, and Africa have become aware of the possibility of development and that they have committed themselves to it and to its consequences is a fact. It creates a momentum that only disaster could reverse. These countries may not succeed in industrializing themselves. But they will, for a historical period at least, give priority to industrial development – and hard times may only accentuate their new awareness of the possibility of, and need for, industrial development.

Similarly, it would take a bold man to predict how fast the Negro will gain complete equality in American society. But that, as a result of the events of 1962 and 1963, there is a new awareness of race relations in the United States on the part of Negro and white alike; above all, that the 'submissive Negro' has become a thing of the past, at least as far as the young people are concerned, is a fact that has already happened. It is the kind of fact that is irreversible. It will have impact; the only question is how soon.

Industry and marketing structures too are areas where the future may have already happened – but where impacts are not yet accomplished.

The Free World economy may collapse again into economic nationalism and protectionism. The tremendous scope and impact of the movement toward a truly international economy in the 1950s and 1960s may have created so much stress and strain (e.g., political pressure from over-protected farmers) that a severe reaction will set in. But the businessman's awareness of the existence and extent of the international economy should persist. It is unlikely, barring catastrophe, that we shall within the next generation fall back into such easy illusions of the 1940s as that this or that industrial region can have something like an unchallengeable economic hegemony, or that a domestic industrial economy can be sealed off from the developments in the world economy. It is unlikely that the many businesses that have gone international these last fifteen years will move back to confining themselves, their operations, and their vision to one national economy and market.

These are – intentionally – big examples. But much smaller changes may also create opportunities to anticipate the future of the business today.

One example of a rather small shift in social and cultural habits that created such an opportunity was the change in the telephone habits of the younger Americans during World War II. Till then long-distance calls were not within the normal behaviour of the great mass of the population; they were for emergencies only. During the war, however, the men in uniform were encouraged to keep in touch with their families through long-distance calls. As a result the long-distance call became normal for the younger war-time generation. It would still be quite a few years before these young people of 1944 would become the heads of families and translate their new telephone behaviour into the normal behaviour of the population. The time could therefore be utilized by the telephone company to carry through a programme of building long-distance facilities and equipment.

The changes that generate the future that has already happened can be found through systematic search. The first area to examine is always population. Population changes are the most fundamental – for the labour force, for the market, for social pressures, and economic opportunities. They are the least reversible in the normal course of events. They have a known minimum lead-time between change and impact: before a rise in the birthrate puts pressure on school facilities, at least five or six years will elapse – but then the pressure will come. And their consequences are most nearly predictable.

By the early 1960s it had become clear that the American population had undergone a drastic change in age structure, in basic cultural habits, and in expectations. While the events that brought this change about had already happened – for by 1961 everybody was already born who would be twenty by 1980 – the impact had not yet begun to make itself felt. It would only begin to be felt in the late 1960s, and would reach its peak in the late 1970s.

By 1977 the American population will be the youngest it has been for 150 years, with at least two-thirds of the population under thirty-five years of age. The median age will be in the middle twenties. But unlike other countries of low average age, life expectancy in the United States is high, with an expected life-span of over seventy for both sexes. Never in history has there been such a relationship between average age and average life expectancy. Whenever in the past we had a young population, life expectancy was also short – and vice versa. What matters is, therefore, not only that people of fairly low chronological age will be the great majority in the American population of the late 1970s, but they will also be people of very low relative or social age; that is, people who by the time they reach median life-span have lived no more than one-third of their life expectancy. This alone should mean tremendous changes in the behaviour and expectations of the American people.

In addition, these young families will have an unprecedented degree of formal schooling. Half of them will contain at least one member, whether man or wife, who has had more than twelve years of schooling. This will mean different expectations on the part of the dominant groups in the labour force. As regards consumer behaviour, we know, for instance, that these couples (the young engineer employed in an electronics company and his wife, for instance) do not buy according to income. They buy according to expectations in respect to their future income and social position. Present income is a restraint on purchases rather than the motivating force.

Few changes in American economic history have been so striking or so fast as this change ahead. It is a change that has already happened.

Yet to my knowledge few if any American businesses have asked themselves: What does this change mean for us? What does it mean for employment and labour force? What does it mean in terms of new markets? How does it change the basic structure of the American market? What does it mean for our customers? Our products? Our entire business posture?

The two fastest-growing markets in the American economy are being created by this population change. But they are not yet to be found in economics books.

First there is an 'activities market' which includes many goods and services hitherto not considered as belonging together: bowling, camping and lawn care but also paperback books and adult higher education. All these activities are in competition with each other. All of them require something scarcer than money: discretionary time. The young engineer or manager who spends his evenings trying to acquire an advanced degree has no time to go bowling or to take care of his lawn. In the activities market, people do not buy to own but to do – in other words, they make no distinction between goods and services. The only distinction they can make is between time they have and time they do not have. The discretionary time market will therefore be both fast growing and rewarding and also competitive and difficult.

The other growth market ahead is the 'office consumption market', i.e., the market for goods and services which, while not going to the individual family (and therefore not traditionally considered consumer goods), also are not used up in the process of production and are, therefore, not traditional producer goods – things like typewriters, computers and all kinds of goods and services to make knowledge workers productive. Again, while rewarding, this is also likely to be a highly competitive and rapidly changing market.

Another field that always should be searched for a future that has already happened is that of knowledge. This search should not, however, be confined to the present knowledge areas of the business. We assume, in looking for the future, that the business will be different. And one of the major areas in which we may be able to anticipate a different business is that of the knowledge resource on which specific excellence of a business is founded. We must therefore look at major knowledge areas, whether they have a direct relation to the present business or not. And wherever we find a fundamental change which has not yet had major impact, we should ask: 'Are there opportunities here which we should and could anticipate?'

The behavioural sciences provide an example of a major change in a knowledge area although few businesses would consider it directly relevant to them. Learning theory is one area in psychology where really new knowledge has been developed these last thirty years. Although this may seem rather remote to businessmen, the new knowledge is likely to have impact not only on the form and content of education but on teaching and learning materials, school equipment and school design, and even on research organization and research management. A wide range of industries – from publishing to construction – might be affected significantly, with great opportunities for those who first convert the potential of the new knowledge into actual goods and services.

One also looks at other industries, other countries, other markets, with the question: Has anything happened there that might establish a pattern for our industry, our country, our market?

In the early 1950s every Japanese electronics manufacturer assumed – quite rationally – that incomes in Japan were too low for television and that the Japanese farmer, in particular, could not possibly afford anything so expensive as a TV set. Most Japanese companies therefore planned for limited production of cheap sets.

Only one small and almost unknown company tried to validate the assumption by looking at what had happened in other countries such as the United States, Great Britan, or Germany. It found that a television set apparently is not considered an ordinary article by the lower-income groups, but offers a satisfaction to them out of all proportion to its cost. In all countries the poor had been the most enthusiastic television customers; they had tended to buy more expensive sets than they could possibly justify by their income status. This one Japanese manufacturer therefore brought out larger and more expensive sets than his competitors. And he aimed a concentrated sales campaign at the Japanese farmer. Ten years later, two-thirds of the low-income households in the Japanese cities and more than half of the farm homes had television, with the larger and more expensive sets in the lead. The formerly small and almost unknown company is now one of the largest Japanese electronics concerns.

Next, one always asks: Is anything happening in the structure of an industry that indicates a major change?

Such a change – now in progress throughout the entire industrial world – is the materials revolution, which erases or blurs the line that traditionally separated different materials streams.

Only a generation ago materials streams were separate from beginning to end. Paper was, for instance, the main manufactured material into which wood could be converted. Paper, in turn, had to be made from a tree. The same situation held for other major materials, aluminium and petroleum, steel and zinc. Most of the finished products coming out of these material streams had specific and unique end-uses. In other words, most substances determined end-uses, and most end-uses determined substances.

Today, however, almost all materials streams are open-ended, first and last. The tree can go into a good many end-products other than paper. Substances that give the same performance as paper can be made from many starting materials other than trees. In respect to end-uses, materials have also become alternatives rather than complements. Paper is on the point of becoming an important material for clothing. There is a wide area of overlap within which products derived from different starting materials can be used to do the same job. Even the process is no longer unique. The paper people increasingly incorporate into their processes techniques developed by the plastics manufacturers and converters; and the textile people increasingly adapt paper industry processes.

Every materials company is aware that its business is changing. A good many companies have done something about the change; the major American can companies have, for instance, bought container manufacturers using glass, paper and plastics. But too few companies have, to my knowledge, realized that the fundamental change is not in their business, or even in business at all, but outside. Where we formerly saw individual substances, we now see materials. The change is so recent that no one can yet define what we mean by 'materials'. But it has already made obsolescent any business that defines itself in terms of one material stream.

Inside the business too there can usually be found clues to events which, while basic and irreversible, have not yet had their full impact.

One indication is often internal friction within the company. Something is being introduced – and it becomes a source of dissension. Unwittingly one has touched a sensitive spot – sensitive often, because the new activity is in anticipation of future changes and therefore in contradiction to the accepted pattern.

Wherever, in an American company, product planning is introduced as a new function and as a specific kind of work, it creates friction. Usually this manifests itself in a long wrangle as to where the new activity belongs. Does it belong in marketing? Or does it belong in research and engineering? Actually, this is much less a dispute over the new function than it is a dim first awareness that the marketing approach tends to make *all* functions secondary and that all functions are cost centres rather than producers of results. This, however, must lead to fundamental changes in organization. It is the anticipation of these changes that makes people react violently to the symptom, product planning.

Top management in the Bell Telephone System set up a new merchandising function ten years or so ago. Very few people in the telephone companies of the systems were affected by it; yet Bell Telephone managers were greatly upset. What had really happened was that the Bell System had attained its major goal of the previous seventy-five years: to equip practically every American home and business with a telephone. Its primary market, the market for the telephone installation, had become saturated. Further growth, therefore, could only be obtained by promoting the maximum use of the telephone rather than by promoting subscriptions to telephone service on a minimum basis. This change that had already happened foreshadowed a radically altered situation in respect to opportunities as well as to risks for the telephone business in the United States; the internal friction over merchandising was only a first symptom.

Any business or activity which has reached its objective is heading into a period of major change. But most people in the business or the activity will continue for a long time to try to achieve the objective that has already been gained. During that period there is a future that has already happened, an opportunity to anticipate.

In the industrially developed countries, for instance, the goal of universal general education has been substantially accomplished. But most educators still think and act on the assumption – valid for the last two hundred years – that the task is to obtain more years of compulsory education. It usually takes a complete generation-shift for the new reality to become widely accepted. But those educational institutions that understand the situation and think through what it makes possible or what it requires will have educational leadership tomorrow.

In business, too, the company that sees that an objective has been reached and acts to redirect its efforts – while its competitors still strain to get to where they already are – will emerge as tomorrow's leader.

Two additional and related questions should be asked: 'What do the generally approved forecasts assert is likely to happen ten, fifteen, twenty years hence? Has it actually happened already?' Most people can imagine only what they have already seen. If, therefore, a forecast meets with widespread acceptance, it is quite likely that it does not forecast the future, but in effect, reports on the recent past.

There is in American business history one famous illustration of the productivity of this approach.

Around 1910, in the early years of Henry Ford's success, the first forecasts appeared that predicted the growth of the automobile into mass transportation. Most people at that time still considered this unlikely to happen before another thirty years or so. But William C. Durant – then a small manufacturer – asked: 'Has this not already happened?' As soon as he asked the question, the answer was obvious: It *had* happened, though the main impact was yet to come. The public's awareness had changed from regarding the car as a toy of the rich to demanding a car for mass transportation. And this would require large automobile companies. On this insight Durant imagined General Motors and began to pull together a number of small automobile manufacturers and small accessory companies into the kind of business that would be able to take advantage of this new market and its opportunity.

The final question should therefore be: 'What are our own assumptions regarding society and economy, market and customer, knowledge and technology? Are they still valid?'

The English middle- and lower-class housewife was well known to be inflexibly conservative in her food-buying and eating habits. The two companies in Great Britain that have emerged in the last ten or fifteen years as leading food distributors, however, raised the question in the late 1940s: Is this assumption still valid? It immediately became clear that the answer was: No. As a result of the food shortages of the war and post-war periods, the formerly conservative English housewife had become used to new foods and new food-distribution methods, and was willing to experiment.

Looking for the future that has already happened and anticipating its impacts introduces new perception in the beholder. The new event is easily visible as the illustrations should have made clear. The need is to make oneself see it. What then could or might be done is usually not too difficult to discover. The opportunities, in other words, are neither remote nor obscure. The pattern, however, has to be recognized first.

As the examples should also have demonstrated, this is an approach of great power. But there is also major danger: the temptation to see as a change what we believe to be happening, or worse, what we believe should happen. This is so great a danger that, as a general rule, any finding should be distrusted for which there is enthusiasm within the company. If everybody shouts, 'This is what we wanted all along,' it is likely that wishes rather than facts are being reported.

For the power of this approach is that it questions and ultimately overturns deeply entrenched assumptions, practices and habits. It leads to decisions to work towards change in the entire conduct, if not in the structure, of the business. It leads to the decision to make the business different.

THE POWER OF AN IDEA

It is futile to try to guess what products and processes the future will want. But it is possible to make up one's mind what idea one wants to make a reality in the future, and to build a different business on such an idea.

Making the future happen also means creating a different business. But what makes the future happen is always the embodiment in a business of an idea of a different economy, a different technology, a different society. It need not be a big idea; but it must be one that differs from the norm of today.

The idea has to be an entrepreneurial one – an idea of wealth-producing potential and capacity, expressed in a going, working, producing business, and effective through business actions and behaviour. It does not emerge from the question: 'What should future society look like?' – the question of social reformer, revolutionary, or philosopher. Underlying the entrepreneurial idea that makes the future is always the question: 'What major change in economy, market, or knowledge would enable us to conduct business the way we really would like to do it, the way we would really obtain the best economic results?'

Because this seems so limited and self-centred an approach, historians tend to overlook it and to be blind to its impact. The great philosophical idea has, of course, more profound effects. But few philosophical ideas have any effect at all. While each business idea is more limited, a large proportion of them are effective. Innovating businessmen have therefore had a good deal more impact as a group than the historians realize.

The very fact that an entrepreneurial idea does not encompass all of society or all of knowledge but just one narrow area makes it more viable. The people who have this idea may be wrong about everything else in the future economy or society. But that does not matter as long as they are approximately right in respect to their own business focus. All that they need to be successful is one small, specific development.

Thomas Watson who founded and built IBM did not see at all the development of technology. But he had the idea of data processing as a unifying concept on which to build a business. This business was, for a long time, fairly small and confined itself to such mundane work as keeping accounting ledgers and time records. But it was ready to jump when the technology came in – out of totally unrelated wartime work – which made data processing actually possible, the technology of the electronic computer. While Watson built a small and unspectacular business in the 'twenties, designing, selling and installing punch-card equipment, the mathematicians and logicians of Logical Positivism (e.g., Bridgman in the United States and Carnap in Austria) talked and wrote a systematic methodology of quantification and universal measurements. It is most unlikely that they ever heard of the young, struggling IBM Company, and certain that they did not connect their ideas with it. Yet it was Watson's IBM and not their philosophical ideas that became operational when the new technology emerged in World War II.

The men who built Sears Roebuck – Richard Sears, Julius Rosenwald, Albert Loeb and, finally, General Robert E. Wood – had active social concerns and a lively social imagination. Yet not one of them thought of remaking the economy. I doubt even that the idea of a mass market – as opposed to the traditional class markets – occurred to them until long after the event. Yet from its early beginnings, Sears Roebuck had the idea that the poor man's money could be made to have the same purchasing power as the rich man's. This was not a particularly new idea. Social reformers and economists had bandied it around for decades. The co-operative movement in Europe largely grew out of it. But Sears was the first business built on the idea in the United States. It started out with the question: 'What would make the farmer a customer for a retail business?' The answer was simply: 'He needs to be sure of getting goods of the same dependable quality as do city people at the same low price.' At the time this was an innovating idea of considerable audacity.

Great entrepreneurial innovations have been achieved by converting an existing theoretical proposition into an effective business.

The entrepreneurial innovation that has had the greatest impact converted the theoretical proposition of the French social philosopher Saint Simon into a bank. Saint Simon starting from Say's concept of the entrepreneur, developed a philosophical system around the creative role of capital. The idea became effective, however, through a banking business:

the famous Credit Mobilier, which his disciples, the Brothers Pereire, founded in Paris in the middle of the nineteenth century. The Credit Mobilier was to be the conscious developer of industry through the direction of the liquid resources of the community. It became the prototype for the entire banking system of the then underdeveloped continent of Europe – beginning with the France, Holland and Belgium of the Pereires' day. The Pereires' imitators then founded the 'business banks' of Germany, Switzerland, Austria, Scandinavia and Italy which became the main agents for the industrial development of their countries. After the Civil War the idea crossed the Atlantic. The American bankers who developed American industry – from Jay Cooke and the American Credit Mobilier that financed the transcontinental railroad, to J. P. Morgan – were all imitators of the Pereires, whether they knew it or not. So were the Japanese Zaibatsu, the great banker-industrialists who built the economy of modern Japan.

The most faithful disciple of the Pereires, however, has been Soviet Russia. The idea of planning through the controlled allocation of capital comes directly from the Pereires; all the Russians did was to substitute the State for the individual banker. (A step taken by an Austrian, Rudolf Hilferding, who started out in Vienna as a banker in the 'business bank' tradition and ended as the leading theoretician of German democratic socialism. His book, *Finance Capital* [1910] was acknowledged by Lenin to have been the source of his planning and industrialization concepts.) There is nothing of this in Marx, above all no 'planning'.

Every single development bank started today in an underdeveloped country is still a direct descendant of the original Credit Mobilier. Yet the Brothers Pereire did not start out to remake the economy. They started a business with the idea of making a profit.

Similarly, the modern chemical industry grew out of the conversion of an already existing idea into a business.

By all odds the modern chemical industry should have arisen in England. In the mid-nineteenth century, England with her highly developed textile industry was the major market for chemicals. It also had the scientific leadership at the time – the time of Faraday as well as of Darwin. The modern chemical industry did actually start with an English discovery: Perkin's discovery of aniline dyes (1856). Yet, twenty years after Perkin – that is, around 1875 – leadership in the new industry had passed to Germany. German businessmen contributed the entrepreneurial idea that was lacking in England: the results of scientific inquiry – organic chemistry in this case – can be directly converted into marketable applications.

The idea on which a business might grow to greatness can be a much simpler one, of course.

The most powerful private business in history was probably the Japanese House of Mitsui, which before its dissolution after Japan's defeat in World War II is said to have employed a million people all over the world. (This at least was the official estimate of the American occupation authorities who decreed the dissolution of the Mitsui concern.) Its origin was the world's first department store, developed in Tokyo in the mid-seventeenth century by an early Mitsui. The entrepreneurial idea underlying this business was that of the merchant as a principal of economic life, rather than as mere middleman. This meant on the one hand fixed prices to the customer. On the other hand, Mitsui no longer acted the agent dealing with craftsman and manufacturer. He would buy for his own account and give firm orders for standardized merchandise to be made according to his specifications. In overseas trade the merchant had acted as a principal all along. Around 1650 however, overseas trade had just been suppressed in Japan – whereupon Mitsui took the overseas-trade concepts and built a domestic merchant-business on them.

The basic entrepreneurial idea may be merely imitation of something that works well in another country or in another industry.

When Thomas Bata, the Slovak shoemaker, returned to Europe from the United States after World War I, he had the idea that everybody in Slovakia and the Balkans could have shoes to wear as everybody had in the United States. 'The peasant goes barefoot,' he is reported to have said, 'not because he is too poor, but because there are no shoes.' What was needed to make this vision of a shod peasant come true was a supply of cheap and standardized, but well-designed and durable footwear, as there was in America. On this analogy Bata built in a few years Europe's largest shoe business and one of Europe's most successful companies.

To make the future happen one need not, in other words, have a creative imagination. It is work rather than genius – and therefore accessible in some measure to everybody. The man of creative imagination will have more imaginative ideas, to be sure. But that the more imaginative idea will actually be more successful is by no means certain. Pedestrian ideas have at times been successful; Bata's idea of applying American methods to making shoes was not very original in the Europe of 1920, with its tremendous interest in Ford and his assembly line. What mattered was his courage rather than his genius.

To make the future happen one has to be willing to do something new. One has to be willing to ask: What do we really want to see happen that is quite different from today? One has to be willing to say: 'This is the right thing to happen as the future of the business. We will work on making it happen.'

'Creativity,' which looms so large in present discussions of innovation, is not the real problem. There are more ideas in any organization, including businesses, than can possibly be put to use. What is lacking, as a rule, is the *willingness to look beyond products to ideas*. Products and processes are only the vehicle through which an idea becomes effective. And, as the illustrations should have shown, the specific future products and processes can usually not even be imagined.

When DuPont started the work on polymer chemistry out of which Nylon eventually evolved, it did not know that man-made fibres would be the end-product. DuPont acted on the assumption that any gain in man's ability to manipulate the structure of large, organic molecules – at that time in its infancy – would lead to commercially important results of some kind. Only after six or seven years of research work did man-made fibres first appear as a possible major result area.

Indeed, as the IBM experience shows, the specific products and processes that make an idea successful often come out of entirely different and unrelated work. But the willingness to think in terms of the general rather than the specific, in terms of a business, the contributions it makes, the satisfactions it supplies, the market and the economy it serves, comes hard to the average businessman.

Moreover, the businessman often lacks the courage to commit resources to such an idea. The resources that should be invested in making the future happen should be small, but they must be of the best. Otherwise nothing happens.

The greatest lack of the businessman is, however, a touchstone of validity and practicality. An idea has to meet rigorous tests if it is to be capable of making the future of a business.

It has to have operational validity. Can we take action on this idea? Or can we only talk about it? Can we really do something right away to bring about the kind of future we want to make happen?

Sears Roebuck with its idea of bringing the market to the isolated American farmer could show immediate results. But DuPont with its idea of polymer chemistry could only organize research work on a small scale; all it could do was to underwrite the research of one first-rate man. Both, however, could *do* something right away.

To be able to spend money on research is not enough. It must be research directed toward the realization of the idea. The knowledge sought may be general – as was that of DuPont's project. But it must be reasonably clear at least that if available, it would be applicable knowledge.

The idea must also have economic validity. If it could be put to work right away in practice, it should be able to produce economic results. We may not be able to do what we would like to see done – not for a long time, perhaps never. But if we could do it now, the resulting products, processes, or services would find a customer, a market, an end-use, should be capable of being sold profitably, should satisfy a want and a need.

The idea itself might aim at social reform. But unless a business can be built on it, it is not a valid entrepreneurial idea. The test of the idea is not the votes it gets or the acclaim of the philosophers. It is economic performance and economic results. Even if the rationale of the business is social reform rather than business success, the touchstone must be ability to perform and to survive as a business.

Businesses started to bring about social rather than economic results are not numerous – though some of the most successful entrepreneurs were primarily reformers in their outlook and approach (Robert Owen, for instance, or the young Henry

Ford). But wherever an attempt succeeds in attaining a social goal through a business, it is because the test of economic validity is applied ruthlessly.

This is being done today, for instance, by Murray Lincoln of the Nationwide Insurance Companies. Describing himself as 'Vice-President in Charge of Revolution', Lincoln has dedicated his life to the advancement of the co-operative movement. He has little good to say of profit-making enterprise. Yet he has tried to promote co-operation through businesses – insurance companies and financial businesses by and large – and he demands of them better business performance than their more orthodox competitors among profit-seeking companies demand of themselves.

Finally, the idea must meet the test of personal commitment. Do we really believe in the idea? Do we really want to be that kind of people, do that kind of work, run that kind of business?

To make the future demands courage. It demands work. But it also demands faith. To commit ourselves to the expedient is simply not practical. It will not suffice for the tests ahead. For no such idea is foolproof – nor should it be. The one idea regarding the future that must inevitably fail is the apparently 'sure thing', the 'riskless' idea, the one 'that cannot fail'. The idea on which tomorrow's business is to be built must be uncertain; no one can really say as yet what it will look like if and when it becomes reality. It must be risky: it has a probability of success but also of failure. If it is not both uncertain and risky, it is simply not a practical idea for the future. For the future itself is both uncertain and risky.

Unless there is personal commitment to the values of the idea and faith in them, the necessary efforts will therefore not be sustained. The businessman should not become an enthusiast, let alone a fanatic. He should realize that things do not happen just because he wants them to happen – not even if he works very hard at making them happen. Like any other effort, the work on making the future happen should be reviewed periodically to see whether continuation can still be justified both by the results of the work to date and by the prospects ahead. Ideas regarding the future can become investments in managerial ego, too, and need to be carefully tested for their capacity to perform and to give results. But the people who work on making the future also need to be able to say with conviction: 'This is what we really want our business to be.'

It is perhaps not absolutely necessary for every business to search for the idea that will make the future. A good many businesses and their managements do not even make their present business effective – and yet the companies somehow survive for a while. The big business, in particular, seems to be able to coast a long time on the courage, work and vision of earlier executives.

But tomorrow always arrives. It is always different. And then even the mightiest company is in trouble if it has not worked on the future. It will have lost distinction and leadership – all that will remain is big-company overhead. It will neither control nor understand what is happening. Not having dared to take the risk of making the new happen, it perforce took the much greater risk of being surprised by what did happen. And this is a risk that even the largest and richest company cannot afford and that even the smallest business need not run.

To be more than a slothful steward of the talents given in his keeping, the executive has to accept responsibility for making the future happen. It is the willingness to tackle purposefully this, the last of the economic tasks in business enterprise, that distinguishes the great business from the merely competent one, and the business builder from the executive-suite custodian.

PART III

A PROGRAMME
FOR PERFORMANCE

12

The Key Decisions

Decisions are made and actions are taken at every step in the analysis of a business and of its economic dimensions. Insights are 'bled-off' and converted into tasks and work assignments. At every step of the analysis there should be measurable results.

But for full effectiveness all the work needs to be integrated into a unified *programme for performance*.

To make the present business effective may require one specific course of action. To make the future of the business different may require different action. Yet what is done to make the present business effective inevitably commits resources, inevitably moulds the future. What is done to anticipate the future inevitably affects the present business in all its policies, expectations, products, and knowledge efforts. Major actions in every one of the economic dimensions have therefore to be consistent with one another. Conflicts between the conclusions of the various analyses have to be reconciled. There has to be balance between the efforts. Otherwise, one effort undoes what another has been trying to achieve. The hard reality of the present must not be obscured by the lure of tomorrow's promises. But the difficult and discouraging work for tomorrow must also not be smothered by the urgencies of the present.

All the work decided upon is work to be done today. It has to be done with the same presently available resources of men, knowledge and money, whether the results are expected soon or in the distant future.

Therefore one set of key decisions must be made for the business in all of its dimensions. These decisions are:
1. The idea of the business;
2. The specific excellence it needs;
3. The priorities.

THE IDEA OF THE BUSINESS

Every company has an idea of its business: a picture of itself and of its specific capacities. Every business sees a specific contribution for which it expects to get paid. This may express itself in nothing more elaborate than the statement, 'This is not our kind of business,' or 'This is not how we do things around here'. It may also be expressed in a voluminous statement of objectives. But there is always an idea that determines how the decision-making people see the business, what course of action they are willing to pursue, and what actions seem to them alien or inconceivable.

The idea of the business always defines a satisfaction to be supplied to the market or a knowledge to be made effective in economic performance. The idea of the business thereby also defines the area in which a company has to obtain and to hold a leadership position.

An apparently simple statement such as: 'We supply the office manager with the materials, supplies and equipment the modern office needs' might define the idea of a business. It identifies the market and the contribution to be made to it. It implies that the function of the business is that of the true merchant whose knowledge of customer needs and of goods, sources and performance characteristics enables him to buy for the customer – the office manager in this case – better value than the customer could obtain for himself. It implies further a commitment to leadership in a major segment of the market: to provide superior satisfaction today; to anticipate the needs and wants of the office of tomorrow; and to give the office manager what he considers value.

But the statement says nothing – and should say nothing – about the specific means through which this idea is realized. This might be manufacturing most of the products the office manager buys. It might be acting as a distributor who buys everything he sells. It might even be functioning as a purchasing agent who charges a commission on whatever he buys for the office manager. And what specific products and product lines should be carried at any given time is – and should be – left open. This is to be decided according to time, place and circumstances, and will change as the office, its technology, its labour force, and the main office buyers change.

'Our business is the application of high energy physics to industrial processes' might serve as the central idea. The emphasis here is on specific knowledge. 'To serve those home owners who take pride in their homes and want to take care of them' may be a perfectly adequate statement of the idea behind a home-service magazine.

Here are some concrete examples from large and well-known companies.

'Our business is public service' was the idea on which Theodore Vail built the American Telephone & Telegraph Company (the Bell System) in the early years of the present century. At the time this was near-heresy. That a business was 'affected with the public interest' was a limitation and weakness. But Vail, for instance, not only accepted public regulation but insisted on it as the prerequisite for a privately owned and privately managed public service industry.

'Our business is business development' was the idea of the Brothers Pereire in their Credit Mobilier, as it has been the idea of all their imitators since.

'Our business is to build into products the work and skill of grocer and housewife' is the idea that underlies every successful processed-food business.

To be valid such a definition should be sufficiently broad to allow the business to grow and to change. Otherwise it may become obsolete at the first change in market or technology. 'Our business is television sets' is too narrow. But 'our business is entertainment' is too general. The idea of the business should enforce concentration. It should make possible determination of the specific knowledges in which excellence has to be attained, and of the specific markets in which the business has to strive for leadership. A valid idea makes it possible for the people in a company to say, 'This fits and should be looked at,' and 'This does not fit and we should not do it.' In other words, it gives *direction* to the business.

An idea of the business needs to be operational. It must lead to action conclusions such as: 'What we need is product development that is likely to result in both a saleable piece of equipment and a constant demand for proprietary supplies to run the equipment.' Or: 'We look for products and processes that fit our marketing organization and distributive skill. Products and processes that do not fit easily will normally be developed only to the point where we can sell or license them to others.' Or, to cite an additional example: 'We are not so much interested in what specific area of technology applies to a project but whether capacity for systems design and systems management is essential to it.'

One of the most important operational conclusions from the idea of the business might be a decision on size. Should the company try to become a large company? Or is it better off remaining fairly small, at least in relation to its market and its competitors. (There are no absolutely large or absolutely small businesses; size is always relative to market and to competition.) A business that aims at growth follows different policies, and requires a different management, from one that can best perform by staying small.

A company that cannot define itself in a valid idea has become amorphous and is likely to try so many things as to be unmanageable.

This applies particularly to businesses which can define themselves only in such broad generalities that they do not specify the areas of excellence needed. The 'electrical industry' or the 'chemical industry' are generalities which no longer serve – however meaningful they were fifty or sixty years ago. 'Transportation' or 'communications' are also so broad as to be meaningless. If such an all-embracing term is the only available definition, the business is doing too many things to do any one thing well.

As long as there are a few major units each of which can be set up and run as a distinct business with a specific and meaningful idea of its own, they can still be managed as one company with the knowledge, direction and purpose. When, however, a company has become a heterogeneous collection that neither serves common markets nor applies excellence in a small number of knowledge areas, it becomes unmanageable. Sooner or later it will become unmanaged. In the first serious test of economic performance and viability – that is, in the first crisis – it will find itself in trouble.

Inability to develop a valid idea of the business is therefore a danger signal. It either indicates a degree of specialization which is irrelevant to market and customer; or it indicates meaningless splintering of knowledge and effort rather than true diversification which multiplies the results of common knowledge and effort. (Specialization and diversification will be further discussed in the next chapter.)

An idea of a business which does not satisfy requirements of validity is always the wrong definition.

But the only positive test is the test of experience.

The idea of the business sums up the answers to the questions that have been asked repeatedly in this book.

What is our business?

What should it be?

What will it have to be?

It establishes *objectives*, it sets goals and direction. It determines what results are meaningful and what measurements truly appropriate.

WHAT IS OUR EXCELLENCE?

Closely related to the idea of the business is the determination of the excellence that characterizes it. This is always knowledge excellence, a capacity of people to do something in such a manner as to give leadership to the enterprise. Identifying the excellence of a business therefore determines what its truly important efforts are and should be.

Very different definitions of excellence can be equally valid, as shown by the experience of many large successful companies.

As was discussed in Chapter 7, General Motors, for instance, clearly prizes excellence in business development and business management. At General Electric, on the other hand, people were for many years encouraged not to concern themselves with business, but to excel as scientists or engineers. IBM, until recently, stressed the ability to produce sales and customers, with the district sales manager the key man.

There is no test except experience by which to judge a definition of excellence. There are, however, tests to identify the invalid definitions.

The definition has to be broad enough to allow for flexibility, growth, and change, and specific enough to allow for concentration. A company which defines its excellence in terms of a narrow specialty – 'the polymer chemist' for instance or the 'financial analyst' – inflicts anaemia on itself. And a company with excellence requirements that read like the headlines in the classified telephone book – from 'accountancy' to 'zipper repair' – is unlikely even to attain mediocrity in any one area. The only 'universal' accomplishment open to a company (or to an individual) is universal incompetence.

A valid definition of excellence must be operational and lead to action conclusions. It has to be the basis for the decisions on personnel: who is to be promoted and for what; who is to be hired; what kind of people should the company try to attract and what attractions should it hold out to them?

Excellence definitions cannnot be changed very often; the definition is embodied in and expressed through people, their values and their behaviour. But no excellence definition will remain valid forever; it must be periodically reviewed and thought through afresh.

Both General Electric and IBM have had to add to their excellence definitions within the last fifteen years. Changes in size, and especially in markets, made General Electric add business management to its central excellence areas. The computer led IBM to add stress on excellence as a professional scientist and engineer.

Any change in the idea of the business or in its structure, in the market or in the major knowledge areas, may require change in a company's definitions of its specific excellence needs.

THE PRIORITIES

No matter how simple and how well ordered a business, there is always a great deal more to be done than there are resources available to do it. The opportunities are always more plentiful than the means to realize them. There have to be priority decisions or nothing will get done. In these decisions a business expresses its final appraisal of all it knows about itself, its economic characteristics, its strengths and weaknesses, its opportunities and needs.

Priority decisions convert good intentions into effective commitments, and insight into action. Priority decisions bespeak the level of a management's vision and seriousness. They decide basic behaviour and strategy.

Nobody seems to have much difficulty setting priorities. What people find difficult is to decide on 'posteriorities'; that is, on what should not be done. It cannot be said often enough that one does not postpone; one abandons. It is almost always a serious mistake to go back to something no matter how desirable it might have appeared when, some time back, it had to be postponed. This is, of course, why people are so reluctant to set posteriorities.

The principles of maximizing opportunities and resources (as described in Chapter 9) govern the priority decisions. Unless the few really first-rate resources are put full-time on the few outstanding opportunities, priorities have not really been set. Above all the truly big opportunities – those that realize potential and those that make the future – must receive the resources their potential deserves, even at the price of abandoning immediate, seemingly safe, but small ventures.

But the really important thing about priority decisions is that they must be made deliberately and consciously. It is better to make the wrong decision and carry it out than to shirk the job as unpleasant and painful and, as a result, to allow the accidents of the business to set priorities by default.

The key decisions on the idea of the business, its excellence and its priorities can be made systematically or haphazardly. They can be made in awareness of their impact or as an afterthought to some urgent triviality. They can be made by top management or by someone way down the line who, in disposing of a technical detail, actually determines company character and direction.

But somehow, some place, these decisions are always made in a business. Without them no action whatever could really be taken.

There is no formula to yield the 'right' answers for these key decisions. But if given haphazardly and without awareness of their importance they will inevitably be the wrong answers. To have even a chance of being right, the key decisions have to be made systematically. This is one responsibility top management can neither delegate nor leave to others.

13
Business Strategies

Whatever a company's programme—

It must decide what opportunities it wants to pursue and what risks it is willing and able to accept.

It must decide on its scope and structure, and especially on the right balance between specialization, diversification and integration.

It must decide between time and money, between building its own or 'buying' – i.e., using sale of a business, merger, acquisition and joint venture – to attain its goals.

It must decide on an organization structure appropriate to its economic realities, its opportunities and its programme for performance.

RIGHT OPPORTUNITIES AND RIGHT RISKS

A business has to try to minimize risks. But if its behaviour is governed by the attempt to escape risk, it will end up by taking the greatest and least rational risk of all: the risk of doing nothing. There are always good reasons for not doing anything if one starts out searching for the negative. Risks, however important, are not grounds of action, but restraints on action. The actions themselves should be selected so as to maximize opportunities.

What opportunities are available should emerge from the analyses of the economic dimensions of the business. Next, they must be looked at in their totality, sorted out and classified.

There are three kinds of opportunities:

Additive;
Complementary;
Breakthrough.

An *additive opportunity* more fully exploits already existing resources. It does not change the character of the business.

An extension of an existing product line into a new and growing market would be an additive opportunity. The paper manufacturer who extends his marketing from the commercial printer to the office reproduction field avails himself of an additive opportunity – even though his products and his selling methods may need considerable change.

Additive opportunities should rarely be treated as high-priority efforts. The risks should be small, for the returns are always limited. Additive opportunities should not be allowed to take resources away from complementary or breakthrough opportunities.

The *complementary opportunity* will change the structure of the the business. It offers something new which, when combined with the present business, results in a new total larger than the sum of its parts.

The opportunity of establishing a paper company in the plastics field, through acquisition of a number of packaging converters who use both paper and plastics, is a complementary opportunity.

The complementary opportunity will always require at least one new knowledge area in which excellence has to be attained. A complementary opportunity, therefore, demands candid self-appraisal: Are we willing and able to change ourselves so as to acquire support and reward the new excellence?

A large mechanical company went into organic chemistry to exploit some rather exciting advances in the forming and shaping of plastic materials developed in its research laboratory. But it tried to run the chemical business as if it were a mechanical business, with the same kind of people and the same basic rules. Far from producing a profit its substantial investment in the plastics fields only created a market for the competitors. In the end the company liquidated its chemical venture at a considerable loss.

A complementary opportunity always carries with it considerable risk. If it appears 'riskless', it is to be shunned as self-delusion. It is therefore not a big opportunity unless it promises to multiply the wealth-producing capacity of the entire business.

The breakthrough opportinity changes the fundamental economic characteristics and capacity of the business.

The typical example is the removal of restraints discussed in Chapter 10, which always requires a breakthrough but also promises extraordinary results.

A breakthrough opportunity requires great effort. It requires the employment of first-class resources, especially human resources.

It often requires major spending on research and development, if not also substantial capital investment. And the risk is always great.

The minimum return, therefore, has to be correspondingly great – or else this is a small opportunity and not worth pursuing.

The story of the Xerox Corporation – one of the spectacular recent growth companies in the United States – is a break-through story. The process was developed to overcome a major restraint on office reproduction technology. It was first offered to a good many larger companies, all of whom turned it down as too risky and too expensive to develop. The Haloid Corporation (as Xerox was then called) was a pigmy when it picked up the process. Yet it spent some $40 million of borrowed money until it had a process that worked. But then the rewards were extraordinary and came fast.

No company that wants to have a future can afford to slight the breakthrough opportunity. This typically is the opportunity to make the future happen. But the effort needed is so great that the breakthrough, if it is successfully realized, should always be capable of creating a new industry rather than an additional product.

Opportunities can also be classified according to their 'fit' to a company.

One of the leading magazine publishers in the United States, Time Inc., has never succeeded in anything but a mass-distributed magazine for a general audience. Another publisher, McGraw-Hill, has had success only with magazines for limited audiences in particular fields or industries, e.g., chemical engineering. Time Inc. might therefore consider as highly risky, if not as inappropriate, what to McGraw-Hill might appear as fairly easy, and vice versa.

There is no obvious reason why one course of action comes easy to one company and seems to be difficult to another, equally well-managed one. It is however a fact. Opportunities therefore have to be reflected against the experience of a company and against its past successes and failures. If for any reason a company does not seem to be able to do well with a certain kind of opportunity, the odds are against success and the risk is high.

Finally one can ask: Is this the kind of opportunity that would help us to realize our idea of the business? Or would it sidetrack us?

An opportunity that runs counter to the idea of the business might yet be the right opportunity. Incongruence between the idea of the business and a major opportunity may be the first indication that a redefinition of the idea is in order. But otherwise opportunities that sidetrack the business typically carry the one risk one cannot afford to take: that of being unable to exploit success.

Risks too need to be classified. A risk is small or big according to its structure rather than according to its magnitude alone.

There are essentially four kinds of risks:

> The risk one must accept, the risk that is built into the nature of the business.
> The risk one can afford to take.
> The risk one cannot afford to take.
> The risk one cannot afford not to take.

In almost every industry there are genuine *risks that must be accepted* to stay in the business. Often they are risks that in any other business would be considered intolerable.

In developing new systemic drugs – such as a new antibiotic, tranquillizer, or vaccine – there is always the danger of bringing to the market a killer rather than a cure. The Thalidomide tragedy of 1960–62 with its terrible legacy of malformed infants is one example. The lethal inoculations ten years earlier of the first batches of infantile paralysis vaccine is another. In neither case could the tragedy have been prevented. We know far too little about the behaviour of the human body to know how to test systemic drugs for all possible effects.

To have brought out a drug of this kind is near-catastrophe for the manufacturer. It causes deep anguish and wounds his self-respect and self-confidence. For pharmaceutical manufacturers must believe in their mission to help cure or at least alleviate, if they are to be at all successful. Yet this risk has to be taken if one wants to be in today's pharmaceutical industry.

No other business, to my knowledge, would be willing to accept this risk.

Yet other risks – though usually less dramatic ones – are inherent in every business.

To lose money and effort spent in pursuit of an opportunity should always be a *risk one can afford to take*. If the money required is more than a company can lose and survive, it cannot afford the opportunity. With every new venture, one should ask: What is the worst that can happen to us if this should fail entirely? Would it destroy us? Would it cripple us and leave us permanently handicapped? Is this, in other words, a risk we can or cannot afford?

The *risk one cannot afford to take* is, therefore, in part the opposite of the risk one can afford. But there are other risks one cannot afford which are of a different nature. Here belongs, above all, the risk of being unable to exploit success.

The initial request for capital for a new venture is sufficient only if the venture fails completely. If it succeeds at all, it will inevitably require further investment. To be unable to exploit such success because capital is not available is a risk one cannot afford to take. Equally serious – and even more common – is inability to exploit a success because knowledge and market are lacking.

In starting any new venture, one therefore always asks: Could we exploit its success? Can we raise the capital to build a small success into a sizeable business? Do we have the technical and marketing skills to realize the opportunity success would open up? Or will we only create an opportunity for somebody else?

The breakthrough opportunity is the *risk one cannot afford not to take*.

The classical example is the often-told story of General Electric's entry into the atomic energy field shortly after World War II. The company's scientists and engineers were apparently unanimous in rating very low the chances of making atomic energy an economical source of electric power. Nevertheless, General Electric decided that a major producer of energy sources could not take the risk of being left out should atomic power generation develop after all. It invested substantial amounts of money and allocated productive and high-quality human resources to the 'long shot'.

But a risk one cannot afford not to take can only be justified by very high rewards should the effort, after all, pay off.

There is no way to make sure that the right opportunities are chosen. But it is certain that the right opportunities will not be selected unless:

The focus is on maximizing opportunities rather than on minimizing risk.

All major opportunities are scrutinized jointly, systematically, and in respect to their characteristics rather than one by one and in isolation.

The attempt is made to understand which opportunities

and risks fit a particular business, and which are not appropriate.

A balance is struck between the immediate and easy opportunities for improvement and the long-range and difficult opportunities for innovation and for changing the character of the business.

SPECIALIZATION, DIVERSIFICATION, INTEGRATION

Every business needs a core – an area where it leads. Every business must therefore specialize. But every business must also try to obtain the most from its specialization. It must diversify.

The balance between these two determines the scope of a business.

Parents Magazine Enterprises had for thirty-five years been a successful publisher of magazines and books on and for children. In the autumn of 1963 it acquired F. A. O. Schwarz, the best-known American toy retail chain. This did not change its specialization at all. But it diversified the fields in which the company's specialization is utilized.

Unilever also exemplifies balance between specialization and diversification. With five hundred companies operating in more than sixty countries, Unilever is so complicated that few outsiders understand its structure. Its activities range from growing oil-bearing seeds and catching fish to selling all kinds of goods to the ultimate consumer. Yet it is at the same time a highly specialized business with a major concentration in marketing grocery products, from fish and processed foods to soaps and toiletries. Any business within Unilever, whether it is a chain of grocery stores or a fleet of fishing vessels, can be understood in terms of the highly specialized knowledge and competence of a grocery-products business.

By contrast, specialization and diversification in isolation from each other are seldom productive. The business that is only a specialty is rarely much more than the practice of an individual professional or designer. It cannot grow as a rule and is likely to die with the one man. The business that is diversified without specialization or specific excellence becomes unmanageable and eventually unmanaged.

A business needs a central resource. It needs to integrate its activities into one knowledge or one market. It needs one area in terms of which business decisions can be meaningfully made. Unless there is such a core, people in the business soon cease to speak a common language. Management itself loses its touch, does not know what is relevant and cannot make the proper decisions. On the other hand, a business needs diversification of result areas to give it the flexibility needed in a world of rapidly changing markets and technologies.

A company should either be diversified in products, market, and end-uses and highly concentrated in its basic knowledge area; or it should be diversified in its knowledge areas and highly concentrated in its products, markets and end-uses. Anything in between is likely to be unsatisfactory.

Cummins Engine Company exemplifies either balance – and the complete shift from one to the other. For many years the company concentrated successfully on one knowledge area; diesel engines for heavy trucks. In its customers and markets, however, it was widely diversified, selling to truck manufacturers all over the world. But recently the number of independent truck manufacturers has been going down. In a complete reversal of its traditional policy, Cummins in the autumn of 1963, merged with the largest of the remaining independent U.S. manufacturers, the White Motor Company, which also has a substantial business in other equipment using engines, such as light and medium-weight trucks, earth-moving equipment, and so on. Cummins thus shifted from concentration on one type of diesel engine to concentration on one customer, and from diversification in markets and customers to diversification in knowledge and product.

The balance between specialization and diversification largely determines the productivity of a company's resources.

Imbalance between major resources (as discussed in Chapter 10) always means a wrong relationship between specialization and diversification. In every case the solution is a change in which a business either diversifies into additional activities that feed off a common core of concentration and knowledge, or redefines the specialization needed. This was the solution for instance for the small manufacturer who, in order to utilize his highly trained sales force, redefined his business as distribution and shifted his centre of specialization from the plant and the process to marketing and selling.

But even a perfect balance is easily upset, as the Cummins Engine story shows. It always needs to be changed when market and economy change.

The best examples are the classical entrepreneurs, the developers of businesses in an underdeveloped economy. They were the business builders in Europe, the United States and Japan in the nineteenth century. They are the business builders today in Brazil – where the Mattarazzo family, for instance, has elaborated the most diversified entrepreneurial empire – in India, and in many other developing parts of the world. Typically, these entrepreneurs start, control and manage a host of businesses, sugar mills, textile companies, banks, cement plants, small steel fabricating plants, and so on.

They represent in the early stages of development a high degree of specialization in the very scarce knowledge of business development and management. But when an economy grows to maturity, this knowledge ceases to be scarce. Specialized technical and marketing knowledge then become crucial. The single entrepreneur with his widespread interests at first becomes unnecessary and then a burden. He gradually turns into an investor. Eventually he disappears.

The scope of a business also has to be redefined when there is a major change in knowledge. Any change, finally, in the idea of business and its excellence calls for a redesign of the balance of specialization and integration.

Integration is often used as a means to diversify or to concentrate. Forward integration – that is, extension of the business scope towards the market – typically adds diversification.

The paper company that acquired a number of packaging companies to convert the threat of plastics into an opportunity used integration towards the market as a means to diversify without having to go into plastics technology. There are hundreds of similar examples.

Backward integration – that is, integration from the market to manufacturing or from manufacturing into the raw materials – is often a way to concentrate.

Every major aluminium fabricator in the world has integrated backward into making the metal despite the high investment required for an aluminium smelter. The metal itself is usually available in adequate supply, except during wartime shortages. Yet excellence in aluminium fabrication is apparently not enough foundation for a major business.

An additional reason for integration, whether forward or backward, is a disparity between the costs and rewards of certain stages of the economic process.

The paper manufacturer, for instance, who acquires a chain of paper merchants aims at higher average profitability. A paper merchant needs little capital and turns it over fast. In good years a dollar invested in paper manufacturing probably earns a good deal more than a dollar invested in a paper merchant. In poor years, however, the merchant is a better risk, if only because his break-even point is quite low.

The analysis of cost structure and cost stream for the entire economic process is therefore the starting point for decisions concerning integration. That combination of stages in the economic process which gives over the long term the most favourable ratio between costs and revenues is the best integration balance for a business. For this one pays, however, the price of increased rigidity.

Every magazine publisher who integrated backward by building his own printing plant has discovered this. Such a plant is a commitment to a printing process, a circulation figure, a frequency of appearance, a page size, and so on. As long as all these factors remain unchanged, the balance is highly advantageous. But they never stay unchanged for long. And then 'our efficient printing plant' soon becomes a cost centre rather than a revenue centre.

Specialization, diversification and integration are strategies of high impact but also of high risk. They should be subject to two tests: the test of economic results, and the test of economic risk.

The configuration and scope chosen should make the business capable of so much greater performance as to change the characteristics of the business altogether. Two plus two should give a configuration that equals at least five. And the risk incurred if anything changes in market or knowledge, products or process, should be one the business can afford to take.

BUILD OR BUY

The main thrust of development in a business comes from within – and therefore requires time. But up to a point, money can be substituted for time: a business can buy rather than build. And in a few cases where there is neither the time nor the knowledge to build, a business has to resort to finance: sale of a subsidiary business or product line, acquisition, merger, joint venture.

Sale is always to be considered when a business or a product line has come to have more value for somebody else. The main line of business growth may have by-passed a product, for instance.

The time clock business of IBM in the United States no longer fitted a company in which the centre of concentration had shifted from simple mechanical devices to the highly complex electronic technology of the computer. IBM sold the business after World War II.

The most common example of a business that should be sold is the one that has outgrown its management. Typically, this is a business that was founded by one able man and developed by him to respectable size. Its prospects are objectively good, but somehow are not being realized. The reason is always the same: the business has outgrown the philosophy, habit and practices of the founder or his family. Unless the people in charge can change their vision and habits, the business will soon deteriorate.

This 'growth' business that suddenly slows down because its management is incapable of adjusting to growth was a main reason for the New York Stock Exchange crash in the spring of 1962. Wall Street had become intoxicated with growth and searched out companies which had been rapidly expanding. In many cases, however, these companies lacked the management to grow beyond small size. As a result they did not fulfil expectations – and stock prices collapsed.

Time is running out fast on such a business. If allowed to deteriorate for more than a short period, it will go under. The radical cure of sale is usually the only salvation for a business stunted by the incapacity of its management to grow up to the demands of success.

Acquisition or merger are similarly indicated for the business that cannot grow to the right size of its own resources – a problem discussed in Chapter 10. Such a business needs all its revenue to maintain the management imposed on it by the discrepancy between its size and the size requirement of its market or its technology. Only acquisition of another business – or by another business – can bring about the rapid expansion necessary. Or there is the alternative of merger in which two such businesses, each too small, come together and form a new business of the right size.

A joint venture, in which two companies combine as partners to found another independent but jointly-owned third company is often the best way to enter a market different from that of either parent company, or to bring two separate knowledge resources to bear on a new opportunity. Again, building would take too much time.

Joint ventures are, for instance, normally the only way in which a Western company can go into business in an alien culture, such as Japan. This requires a knowledge of the Japanese market, of Japanese traditions – and above all of the Japanese language – which would take a Western company many years to acquire. It requires also technology, product and process knowledge, and technological research which it would take the Japanese a good many years to develop. Each partner, therefore, contributes something unique. The joint venture exploits a different market from that of either partner – different in culture from its Western parent, different in technology and product line from the Japanese parent.

Acquisition is sometimes the best way to change the balance between specialization and diversification. It is often the best way to bring new competence and new knowledge into the business. Merger may be the best way to convert an imbalance of resources into a source of strength. Sale may be the quickest way to put on 'milking status' an old business or an old product line.

The financial tools are, however, difficult and demanding. They cannot be used as substitutes for the development of people and organization, for innovation, or for work on the economic direction and performance of a business. These require internal efforts – and time.

Furthermore, buying time is never cheap. If one buys the time which somebody else has put into knowledge, resources, products, markets, one pays a premium price. Unless the acquisition promises to add a great deal to the business, it will not justify its cost.

Finally, buying time never succeeds unless it is followed by purposeful internal efforts.

The best example is Durant's construction of General Motors entirely through financial acquisition. With the companies he bought, Durant got an array of extraordinarily capable men. But only after Durant's ouster, when Sloan built a company, defined the idea of the business, and developed a management team, did Durant's financial creation become viable. Buying good businesses in a growth industry, each run by a first-class man, by itself had only produced near-disaster.

Every company that has put its trust in financial manipulation as a substitute for purposeful management has eventually come to grief. Using financial tools makes greater demands than development from within on a management, its competence, and its willingness to face up to the hard decisions. Because the financial tools save time and telescope years of growth and development into one legal transaction, they also telescope years of problems and decisions into a very short time. Every merger creates as many problems, especially of people and their relationship, as would have been created by developing a new and larger business from within. There has never been an acquisition which really fitted, and which did not have to be reconstructed before it began to give the expected results. And every joint venture, if successful, raises problems which force the respective parents to change their own habits and expectations.

Thus financial transactions are a tool of business policy. They are not a substitute for it.

Litton Industries, the California-based 'science' company, is perhaps the outstanding post-war example of 'the company that stock deals built'. In ten years, from 1953 to 1963 it grew from nothing to half a billion dollars in sales – all through acquisition. Yet Charles B. Thornton, the man who assembled Litton, was quoted as saying: 'We had to grow big and muscular in a hurry to survive the jolt of changing technology. But we have never acquired companies as such. We have bought time, a market, a product line, a plant, a research team, a sales force.' (*Time*, October 4, 1963.)

Only a management that truly subordinates the financial aspect of these transactions to business policy can ever use financial tools with success. Otherwise all it does is spend money without buying anything with it, least of all time.

STRUCTURE AND STRATEGY

Two recent books* have documented the relationship between organizational structure and the ability of a company to produce results and to grow. Structure, Professor Chandler demonstrates, follows strategy. Miss Penrose makes it equally clear that growth demands the right structure.

The right structure does not guarantee results. But the wrong structure aborts results and smothers even the best-directed efforts. Above all structure has to be such that it highlights the results that are truly meaningful; that is, the results that are relevant to the idea of the business, its excellence, its priorities and its opportunities.

That it spotlights business performance and business results is, of course, one of the main benefits of decentralization (the organization structure under which individual parts of a company are set up as distinct business entities). This, however, requires economic understanding of the business, and indeed continuing work on the economic tasks of each decentralized business and of the company as a whole, performed for the company's top management and at the central office. There is no point in setting up as 'businesses' activities which do not have a distinct product or service for a distinct market and are therefore not truly businesses. Where these two requirements are met, however, decentralization, as Professor Chandler's books shows, is the structure that best serves business performance and growth.

Yet no matter how well suited to the needs of today's business, organization must be reviewed as the business changes. Is division into different components still likely to advance the economic performance of the company as a whole? Or is it likely to make the component's results look good at the expense of the over-all company? Are the efforts in which excellence should be attained organized as distinct responsibilities or are they submerged in a general, unspecified gaggle of mediocrities?

Such structural questions always need to be asked. They are

---

* Edith T. Penrose, *The Theory of the Growth of the Firm* (Oxford: Blackwell, 1960) and Alfred D. Chandler, Jr., *Strategy and Structure* (Cambridge, Massachusetts: M.I.T. Press, 1962). I acknowledge here the stimulation and insights found in both works.

actually more important in the small than the large company – simply because the small company usually pays too little attention to structure. They are particularly pertinent in the company which has undergone a period of rapid growth. Indeed to think through its structure is the best way to prevent such a company from outgrowing its management to the point where only sale of the business can save it.

One job that always needs to be organized as a distinct activity is the economic analysis of the business, its dimensions and tasks, and the programme for performance. It is distinct work. It is crucially important work. And it is a great deal of work. Someone must therefore be assigned to it and must be responsible for it. And except in the smallest business he will have a full-time job on his hands.

All I have tried to do in this chapter is to show that these big areas – opportunity and risk; scope of the business; financial strategies, or organization – should be considered and thought through by management in developing the programme for performance. For the strategic decisions in these four areas will largely determine whether the means chosen by a business are adequate to its aims and ambitions.

14

Building Economic
Performance into a Business

To turn an entrepreneurial programme into performance requires
effective management:

    The programme must be converted into work for which
someone is responsible.

    The programme must be anchored in the practices of the
business.

    The focus on economic performance must be built into
the job of people and into the spirit of the organization.

THE WORK PLAN

Just as there is need for a unified, company-wide programme for
performance, there is need for a unified, company-wide plan for
the work to be done.

The foundations of such a plan are, of course, the decisions on
the idea of the business and its objectives; on the areas of excellence; on priorities; and on strategies. From these a work plan
first derives goals and targets. What results are needed? Where?
When? This then leads to an assessment of the efforts required and
to the selection of the resources to be committed.

Next there are work *assignments*. Performance becomes a job for
which *someone* is responsible. If it is to be a real assignment, there
has to be a deadline; work without deadlines is not work assigned
but work toyed with.

Special attention needs to be paid to planning knowledge work,
which demands more analysis, more direction, and a more sharply
focused plan of action than other work. What a man should be
doing at a machine is usually clear and simple. But a sales manager
sitting at a desk might be doing any number of things. Or he might
be doing nothing, with no one the wiser for a long time. Yet only
in a few businesses is knowledge work thought through and
purposefully directed.

The vague generalities with which knowledge efforts are

typically defined in company manuals and budgets are symptomatic. 'Advice and support to the company's marketing work in all areas' is a popular phrase; 'To improve utilization of human resources on all levels' is another. But why does the marketing effort need 'advice and support'? And what results are expected, and when?

In particular a clear plan, directly focused on the objectives and goals of a business, is needed for the most expensive and most demanding knowledge effort of all: research, whether in technology, in markets, on customers, or in any other areas.

Increasingly businesses need pure research; that is, research aimed at acquiring new, not yet existing knowledge. Such research particularly needs to be focused on economic results. It is more productive the more directed it is in its objectives. Whether it will produce results is, of course, unknown – and the odds are against success. But if there are results, they should be economically applicable ones. The work at DuPont that produced Nylon was pure research. But it was clearly aimed at an economic result, clearly fitted in with DuPont's idea of the business and clearly supported the DuPont objectives. The same was true of the work at Bell Laboratories which led to the transistor, or the work at General Electric out of which came the synthetic diamond. The research in polymer chemistry of the two 1963 Nobel Prize winners, Karl Ziegler of Germany and Giulio Natta of Italy, while of the purest, was from the beginning focused on economic results; that is, on creating new major industries.

It is important in knowledge work not to do things that will not lead to major results, even if done successfully. It is important in knowledge work – and again especially in research – to abandon what is no longer productive and to concentrate the scarce resources where the results are. For knowledge work is productive only when done by people of extraordinary ability. Outstanding people, however, are as scarce in knowledge work as in any other area of human endeavour.

BUSINESS PRACTICES

All proposals for new ventures, capital investment, or new products and services, should be directed towards the company's programme for performance. All such proposals should be presented together rather than piecemeal. This applies to capital investments for a given period, to new products or new services, and to all new activities and efforts, especially knowledge efforts. Only in this way is it possible to find out whether these proposals seek the best utilization of the company's resources and whether they are focused on the right opportunities and on the needed results. Only in this way can it be seen whether the proposed investments, products, or activities aim at realizing the idea of the business and support its objectives.

Each individual proposal should clearly spell out the expectations that underlie it. What is assumed will happen? How do these assumptions compare with the expectations on which the company's programme has been based? What would be the consequences of not making the new investment, not starting the new activity, not turning out the new product?

What would happen to the business should this new venture not succeed? No proposal should be seriously considered unless it presents bluntly and without concealment the worst that could conceivably happen. Equally important are the consequences of success. What are we committed to should this new venture succeed? And is it a commitment we can afford?

Every proposal for a new venture should be focused on the entire company. It is not enough to know what results are expected from the venture itself. What would it add to the total economic capacity and results of the business? Some proposals promise high returns on the capital or effort expended, yet add so little to the total economy of the business as to be inconsequential. There are also proposals which, in their own terms, barely pay their own way, and yet may add substantial capacity for results. What matters most is not the return on a specific venture but its impact on the results of the entire business.

A proposal for any new venture must spell out what resources, especially what human resources, will be needed and where they are to come from. There is no point in going into anything new unless high-quality resources can actually be made available to it.

A proposal for a major new effort should therefore always spell out what old effort will be abandoned. Resources of the necessary calibre for a new effort – especially people of the right calibre –

rarely lie around idle. They have to be made available by abandoning an old effort or at the least by putting it on 'milking status'.

Another necessary business practice is a systematic review of all products (or services), all activities, all major components of the business, every three years or so. This review first holds performance against expectations. It then asks: 'If this product (activity or unit) were not here today, would we start it?' If the answer is: 'No', then the question should be asked: 'Should we continue, and why?'

If we want the new to have a chance, we must be willing to prune the old that no longer promises results. If we want the people in an organization to be 'creative', we must manage the business in such a way that jobs and careers are linked to finding the new and promising rather than to perpetuating the old and outworn, to results rather than to routine.

PEOPLE, THEIR JOBS AND THEIR SPIRIT

Only yesterday the economic decisions even in a very big business were made by a few men at the top. The rest carried them out. Today's reality was concisely described by Frederick R. Kappel – the head of the world's largest privately-owned and privately-managed business, the American Telephone and Telegraph Company – in a talk to the XIIIth International Management Congress, held in New York in September 1963 .

Years ago, when our business was started [said Mr Kappel] it was the vision of the top managers that established the goals of the organization. [Today by constrast] the goals of the business, the visions of the future, are not imposed by top management alone. . . . Our viewpoint is not formed by the business manager alone or by the director of research alone or by the development engineer alone. . . . The responsibility for decision rests with the head of the business but the decision itself is the product of multiple judgement. . . . To enable the knowledge workers to make their contribution, a business therefore needs: (1) a clear view both of what is needed and of what is feasible; (2) a closely reasoned determination of the best course for achieving the desired results; and (3) a dependable measure of the means already available and those that must still be discovered. . . . A business can excite the scientist . . . only if it has a clear idea of what it is aiming at, only if these aims are explicitly stated.

Even the small business today consists increasingly of people who apply knowledge, rather than manual skill and muscle, to work. Every knowledge worker makes economic decisions – whether he be a research engineer deciding to continue or drop a project, an accountant deciding what cost definitions are appropriate to the business, a sales manager deciding where to put his strongest salesmen, or a market researcher defining the market in which a product competes. To make the right decision the knowledge worker must know what performance and results are needed. In turn, the knowledge worker must be 'excited', to use Mr Kappel's word. He cannot be supervised. He must direct, manage and motivate himself. And that he will not do unless he can see how his knowledge and work contribute to the whole business.

It is therefore essential that the job of every managerial and professional member of the organization be defined in terms of the contribution it should make to the attainment of the company's economic results. To define a job in terms of work and skill is adequate for people whose contribution is only faithful effort. For people who have to have knowledge and judgement, self-direction and the 'excitement' that motivates, the emphasis has to be on contribution and results.

If a company is to obtain the needed contributions, it must reward those who make them. The spirit of a company is made, in the last analysis, by the people it chooses for senior positions. Altogether, the one and only true 'control' in any organization is its decisions on people and especially its promotions. They affirm what an organization really believes in, really wants, really stands for. They speak louder than words and tell a clearer story than any figures.

To infuse the spirit of a company with a desire for economic performance requires stress in the crucial promotions on ability for the economic task. Such a promotional policy is largely the 'secret' of those companies – General Motors, DuPont, Sears Roebuck are examples – whose performance has been consistently high.

The crucial promotion is not a man's first – though it may be the most important one to him and to his career. Nor is it the final promotion into a top position; there a management usually must choose from a small, already pre-selected group.

The crucial promotion is into the group from which tomorrow's top people will have to be selected. It is the decision at the point where the pyramid in an organization narrows abruptly. Up to this point there are in a large organization usually forty to fifty men to choose from for every vacant spot. Above it the choice narrows to one out of three or four. Up to this point also, a man usually works in one area or function. Above it he works in the business.

The military has known this for many years. Up to the rank of major, promotion is generally by seniority and depends largely on survival. But of every thirty or forty majors only one can make colonel. And yet only those that get to be colonel have an opportunity to become generals later on, while future generals are selected from a small group of colonels. In the military, therefore, it is at the promotion to colonel that the 'Promotion Board' most carefully screens candidates.

In a business these promotions still lead, as a rule, into jobs that are functional, technical, or in one specific area – head of market research, for instance, assistant chief engineer, or assistant controller. Yet they determine the top management of tomorrow. They are, moreover, the most visible and meaningful promotions for the organization itself, and the ones its people most closely scrutinize. For the men in these positions are the only senior executives with whom most of the managerial professional men in the organization have any close working contact.

If a business is to focus on economic performance it must, therefore, in filling these critical positions, reward men for proven capacity to contribute to the company's goals and results, for demonstrated ability at the economic tasks, and for willingness to work for the business rather than only as specialists in one function or in one technical area.

Capacity for the economic tasks and willingness to work on them is by no means the only requirement for a senior executive. In many positions it is surely not even the most important one, compared, for instance, to the ability to build and lead an effective and cohesive human organization. But for a senior executive understanding of, and sympathy for, the demands of economic performance are essential requirements.

To build business performance into the human organization is difficult. But it is essential. A company, after all, does not have a programme for performance. Its executives have such a programme, work it out, formulate it, make it effective. Economic results are not produced by economic forces; they are a human achievement.

Conclusion:

The Commitment

The important economic decisions today are mainly made by executives – managers employed by a company who work within and through a business organization. They are no longer made by the entrepreneur – an individual operating independently, for himself and by himself.

Organized business has become the entrepreneurial centre of modern economy and society. The economic decisions it makes or forgoes largely determine the level, direction and course of industrial economy.

The traditional entrepreneur has not disappeared. Indeed, the large and expanding industrial economy gives greater scope than any earlier age to the individual who starts a new business by himself and for himself. Since World War II a large number of 'new men', starting from scratch and by themselves, have built new businesses and even whole industries – in the United States, in Western Europe, in Japan, India, Latin America. But even at his most active, this individual entrepreneur is but a small – though essential – element in the economy, compared to the already established and organized businesses. Moreover, the individual entrepreneur has to organize a business and has himself to become an executive as soon as he has any success. Otherwise his entrepreneurial achievement will evaporate in no time. Even a small business in today's economy is in size and complexity so far removed from the biggest and wealthiest individual entrepreneur as to be totally different in kind.

For every business therefore, systematic, purposeful work on economic tasks and decisions has to become a way of life. What the tasks are and how they might be organized has been the concern of this book.

But if the business enterprise is the entrepreneurial centre of a modern economy, every knowledge worker in it has to act the entrepreneur. In the modern business in which knowledge is the central resource, a few people at the top cannot by themselves assure success. The more business becomes a knowledge organization the more executives there will be whose decisions have impact on the whole business and its results.

Top management does not thereby become less important nor does its job become less demanding. On the contrary, it has acquired a new and challenging dimension to its task: leading, directing, motivating the knowledge-people to become effective executives.

The man of knowledge in business – whether manager or individual professional contributor – has to impose on himself the executive's threefold commitment:

A commitment to make his knowledge and efforts *contribute* to economic results. The knowledge worker's focus has to be on contribution rather than on the work, its skills and its techniques.

A commitment to *concentrate*. Each knowledge worker, to be an executive, needs to take responsibility for allocating to opportunities and results the one resource truly under his control: himself.

A commitment finally, to the *systematic*, *purposeful* and *organized* discharge of the economic tasks in his own job and work as well as in the total business.

There is a great deal of stress today on the social responsibilities of the manager. The knowledge workers in business enterprise – manager and individual professional contributor – have emerged as a new leadership group in industrial society. And every leadership group has indeed responsibilities well beyond its own immediate task and scope.

But the first social responsibility of the manager today is to make understandable to the laymen – the educated people who are outside of business and necessarily ignorant of it – what it is that business does, can do and should do, and what it is the manager is doing.

A good deal of what looks like 'hostility to business' is in fact nothing but the bafflement of the educated layman – the professional man, the civil servant, the academician – at an activity which apparently can neither be studied nor explained. Mr Nehru and his generation, for instance, became 'socialists' primarily because of the contempt of their intellectual masters, the English Fabians of the early 1900s, for what they saw when they looked at the business of their day: a seemingly mindless game of chance at which any donkey could win provided only that he be ruthless. But that is, of course, how *any* human activity looks to the outsider unless it can be shown to be purposeful, organized, systematic; that is, unless it can be presented as the generalized knowledge of a discipline.

Managers have become a leadership group in the last two decades largely because they have developed such a discipline for the managerial half of their job: the planning, building and leading of the human organization of a business. But for the other, the entrepreneurial half – the half that deals with the specific and unique economic function of business enterprise – the systematic discipline has yet to be evolved. All over the world executives have committed themselves to management as a discipline. Now they have to commit themselves to purposeful entrepreneurship. Only when entrepreneurship is presented as a discipline and practised as the specific task that systematically directs resources to economic performance and results, will an educated layman be able to understand what business – industrial society's economic organ – is trying to do, and to respect what it is doing. Only then can society truly accept that business is a rational pursuit and that the executive in business has an important contribution to make.

For his own sake too the knowledge worker needs the commitment to contribution, concentration, and purposeful entrepreneurship. He needs it to make meaningful and satisfying his own life and work. More and more knowledge people work in business. Indeed, modern business is the biggest source of jobs that allow men to put knowledge to productive use. The knowledge worker in whom so much expensive education has been invested should be held to high demands for effort and performance. But he also should make high demands on the job for satisfaction and stimulation.

The economic task, if done purposefully, responsibly, with knowledge and forethought, can indeed be exciting and stimulating, as this book has, I hope, conveyed. It offers intellectual challenge, the reward of accomplishment, and the unique enjoyment man derives from bringing order out of chaos.

Bibliography

There is no book so far that attempts to cover the entire field of economic decisions and tasks in business enterprise. There are in fact few books that have other than narrowly technical and functional concerns. Among those few I have found the following to be stimulating and of interest:

MAJOR ECONOMIC DECISIONS

Chandler, Alfred D., Jr. *Strategy and Structure* (Cambridge, Mass.: M.I.T. Press, 1962).

Penrose, Edith T. *The Theory of the Growth of the Firm* (Oxford: Blackwell, 1960).

IMPORTANT TOOLS OF ECONOMIC ANALYSIS

Dean, Joel. *Managerial Economics* (Englewood Cliffs, N.J.: Prentice-Hall, 1951).

Rautenstrauch, Walter and Villiers, Raymond. *The Economics of Industrial Management*, 2nd ed. (New York: Funk & Wagnalls, 1957; London: Mayflower Press, 1958).

Spencer, Milton and Siegelman, Louis. *Managerial Economics: Decision Making and Forward Planning* (Homewood, Ill.: Richard D. Irwin, 1962).

FINANCIAL MANAGEMENT

Garner, Fred V. *Profit Management and Control* (New York: McGraw-Hill Book Company, 1955).

Solomon, Ezra (ed.). *The Management of Corporate Capital* (Glencoe, Ill.: The Free Press, 1959).

Solomon, Ezra. *The Theory of Financial Management* (New York: Columbia University Press, 1963).

Weston, J. F. *Managerial Finance* (New York: Holt, Rinehart & Winston, 1962).

PLANNING

Ewing, David (ed.). *Long-Range Planning for Management*, rev. ed. (New York: Harper & Row, 1964).

LeBreton, Preston P. and Henning, Dale A. *Planning Theory* (Englewood Cliffs, N.J.: Prentice-Hall, 1961).

Payne, Bruce. *Planning for Company Growth* (New York: McGraw-Hill Book Company, 1963).

Index